No Greater Joy Volume Two

by
Michael & Debi Pearl

Published by
No Greater Joy Ministries
1000 Pearl Road
Pleasantville, TN 37033
United States of America

No Greater Joy Volume Two®
Copyright © 1999 by Michael Pearl
ISBN 1-892112-07-8
First printing: April 1999
Third printing: February 2005

This title is also available as a No Greater Ministries Inc. audio product.
Visit www.nogreaterjoy.org for more information.

Requests for information should be addressed to:
No Greater Joy Ministries Inc. *1000 Pearl Road, Pleasantville, TN 37033 USA*

The Cover

The beautiful artwork on the cover is entitled "Grand Adventure," by Mark Keathley. Limited Edition Prints of this image and other Artworks by Mark Keathley may be obtained from NEWMARK, USA, 11700 Commonwealth Drive, Louisville, KY 40299. (800) 866-5566

Table of Contents

Preface

Our first book on child training, **To Train Up a Child,** has now been distributed in a quantity approaching 400,000. In answer to the many questions we receive in the mail, Deb and I began the publication of a newsletter, **No Greater Joy.** It started out as eight pages but soon grew to twenty-four. It is now distributed to over 45,000 homes.

We found that most of the questions we were asked had already been answered in one of our previous newsletter articles. The demand for back newsletters was so great that it became a burden to maintain an inventory. Thus, we compiled our second book on child training, **No Greater Joy Volume One.**

But the letters continued to come in, and new issues were raised or old ones needed further attention. More newsletter articles were written. So now we give you a further compilation of articles in this: **No Greater Joy Volume Two.**

It is a provocative experience to read the many letters we receive daily. One letter will tear at our souls as we read of the pain and injury occurring in a family. The next letter will thrill us with wonder at the miracles God has accomplished in a parent's heart. Debi and I are always discussing, analyzing, praying, and writing. Much has been written that we are not yet ready to make public. In time, as our hearts are settled and our key boards express our minds, we will address a broader scope of family issues.

We pray that in this volume you will find a little light to direct your steps in the most important job in all of human history—training up a child in the way he should go.

Training Roseanna's Flesh

T welve-month-old Roseanna has one adoring mama, one adoring daddy, one adoring five-year-old sister, one adoring seven-year-old brother, and dozens of adoring friends. But Roseanna has one enemy—her flesh. Like all one-year-olds, her "wanter" is growing faster than her winning smile. Her accomplices, the adults and children around her, are disarmed by her charming ways. To supply her needs and wants, and in so doing win her gratitude, is an occupation to which most adults would blindly surrender with religious devotion. It is hard not to "worship" such innocence and beauty.

The very young and yet uncontaminated of our species turn us mature, reserved adults into silly court jesters. We drop our social guard as if we were in our own private thought life. We can be too tired to serve our spouses, and yet be suddenly filled with energy to jump up and gratify these little angels. In our servitude to the baby, we are meeting our own needs, which often results in the real needs of the child being overlooked.

Deb recounts an experience that occurred one fall when we camped out in the Rocky Mountains with several families:

"I spent a good portion of each day cooking around the camp fire. Roseanna's brother and sister, Jubal and Beulah, were often huddled around our campfire. I enjoyed showing them all kinds of fun things, like baking potatoes under the ashes and hot coals, or making a bellows to get our fire hotter when we wanted to bend some metal. One day someone mentioned starting a fire without matches, and I remembered I had a magnifying glass with me. I allowed each child to take a turn focusing the magnified sun spot on his/her skin to feel it warm up. Roseanna, seeing everyone's interest in the little object, decided it was worth investigating. She wiggled herself into the middle of the gang and grabbed the glass away from her sister. Beulah is a sweet child and was willing to give-in to her younger sister. But I saw that Roseanna's flesh needed to learn self-discipline. So I took the glass away from her and gave it back to Beulah. Roseanna looked at me like I was a mean, over-sized kid. She defiantly grabbed the glass. 'No,' I spoke firmly, and again took the glass. Really, it did seem rather mean; after all, she was just a curious baby. I wanted her to like me, and Beulah would understand if I let the baby have it. But I persevered until Roseanna yielded to my will."

It would have been no discomfort or inconvenience to allow Roseanna to examine the magnifying glass for a minute. But if you wait until actions become irritating before you discipline, you have allowed them to confirm selfish habits that are then hard to break. You must begin training before the need to discipline arises. There will be fifty occasions a day where you will want to train your one-year-old. An occasion for training is not determined by our concern for what the child is or isn't doing; the issue is to make sure that the child is never allowed to gain an advantage through selfish grabbing, whining, stubborn refusal, etc. IT IS A MATTER OF ESTABLISHING AN UNDERSTANDING OF WHO IS IN CONTROL. You must look for opportunities to demonstrate that you have the last word, that your authority is to be obeyed without question. This is not done by punishing the child. If you are consistent, the assertion of your authority will be such a non-event that others looking straight at you will never know anything occurred.

For example: a child tries to slide from your lap onto the floor. On most occasions that's just a way of letting you know where he wants to go. Fine. But there are times when you do not want him to slide to the floor. If your little fourteen-month-old makes an attempt to dismount your lap, and you indicate that you do not want him to, and he makes a protest by jerking away or whining, then by no means can you allow him to intimidate you into compliance. By so doing you have allowed the authority to pass to him. You would be encouraging rebellion. YOU MUST ALWAYS BE PERCEIVED TO WIN ANY CONTEST. It is all determined by what the child thinks. If there is a seed of resistance in the child, it must never be allowed to grow. Don't allow that spirit of rebellion to become profitable.

When the child whines and makes an issue of something that to you was otherwise irrelevant, you must then follow through, causing the child to do what he did not want to do. This is soul training—character building—sanctification of the natural spirit in your child. This won't make him a Christian, but it will give him a better character than most Christians possess.

If, during the course of a day, no contest arises naturally, you should arrange one. Seek opportunity to thwart the child's will, to cause him to submit to your command. If you cause him to surrender his will to you twenty times during the course of a day, he will not disappoint you with disobedience in public. Tell him to stop, sit, don't speak for five minutes, etc. Play the half-hour "quiet time game," the half-hour "don't wiggle and squirm game." Refuse him a treat when he is wanting it badly. Give it to him only when he is joyously submitted to your timetable. You mustn't give the appearance of being blindly arbitrary, but always maintain full control. Never allow the child to dictate your actions.

Just yesterday, a little four-year-old was visiting the house. I (Michael) was eating cake when he came in from playing. He asked for some, and I said, "OK." But I delayed for a few seconds while I was finishing a bite. Before I made a move to rise, he somewhat impatiently said, "I am hungry now." That did it! Time for training. Rather than proceed as I had planned, rising to get his cake so we could eat together, I said, "Well, you will just have to wait until I get through."

By surrendering to his demand I would have cultivated impatience in the little fellow. It took me three times as long to eat the cake—while he sat two feet away drooling on the table. I never lectured him or rebuked him in any way. Just waiting on me was sufficient training in patience and respect for the rights of others.

The older children should be taught through example to also participate in training the younger children. When a six-year-old can responsibly train a one-year-old, it is a two edged sword. You are confirming the training of the six-year-old while also training the six-year-old to be a good parent.

If you are in the middle of raising a family, yet just now instituting proper training, you will have added struggles for awhile. If you are demonstrating your authority over the two-year-old, while the

six- and eight-year-old are still permissive, it will send mixed sig-
nals to the younger children. You must discuss it with them and ask
for their help. They feel much as you do about a spoiled little sister.
They would love to see her brought under control. If they assist you
and see positive results, you have also trained them indirectly. Once
a child understands the principle behind your consistent demands,
he will appreciate your intentions. It then becomes much easier,
because the children will cooperate rather than resist. Of course, to
be effective, a cheerful, self-possessed attitude on your part is an
absolute must.

What is our purpose as parents in establishing our authority?
Your child's flesh is growing faster than his soulish faculties. The
understanding will mature several years behind the passions of the
body. If you wait until children are old enough to see and appreciate
the need to exercise self-control (as Paul said, "mortify the deeds of
the body"), by that stage of their lives they are thoroughly bound in
the habits of self-indulgence. By the time they see the need to deny
the flesh, the flesh has thoroughly established itself as tyrant over
soul and spirit. Using Scriptural terms: our job as parents is to cultivate the "inner man" of the children and teach them to deny the
"outer man."

Last week in the church meeting I noticed a young mother training her little girl to be indulgent and intemperate. The baby was
discontent, a grouch, and the mother was taking the easiest path to
purchasing some quiet. The child obviously wasn't hungry, but the
mother was using a bottle to pacify her. They were playing a game
of "shove and retrieve." Mother would alternately shove the bottle
into the mouth of the demanding baby and then retrieve it when it
was nearly cast away. This hour of squirming, grouching, and bottle
pacifying was cultivating self-indulgence in the child.

Now you say, "But what can a mother do in a public place?"
Not much, if she hasn't prepared for it by consistently training at
home.

Public places don't make unruly kids, they just expose
"untraining" parents. If you are loose at home, the kids will be loose
in public. Don't go to a public place and make a scene by carrying
your child out to spank him. The impression you leave is not what
you think.

I know that most of you that have problems in this area have just been unaware of the high possibilities. You are not lazy or indifferent, quite the contrary; you are ready and willing to do all that you know to do. We hope to have raised your level of expectation, to have expanded your vision.

One final warning: Our enemy is distraction, leading to neglect. Focus, and determine to concentrate on that which is most important to you, your children. Ask God to show you how to organize your own life, right down to your thoughts, so you can apply yourself to that which will reach into eternity—your child's soul. ☺

Dear Michael and Debi Pearl,

Why didn't I figure this all out before? It is so easy! It must be a spiritual deception. Your books have blessed us beyond measure. I no longer am angry at my children for being untrained. Now I acknowledge my responsibility to train them and to train myself! I am getting under submission to my husband and everyday is a new adventure. We have 8 children and our house is peaceful and fun, even when it is loud with jubilant little voices.

Many Thanks

K.G. from MO.

Mr. & Mrs. Pearl,

Thank you ever so much for sharing your God-given wisdom with others! Our family is happier, healthier, and (praise God!) holier because of the principles for family life from your books!   T. A.

An Idea We Tabled

U ntil recently, our family didn't sit down at a table, we sat down at a continent. My wife bought a perfectly clear table cloth and under it she placed several large world and national maps. We grew fond of quizzing each other on obscure countries now owned by ex-CIA operatives. My boys came to know the rivers and mountain ranges of different countries.

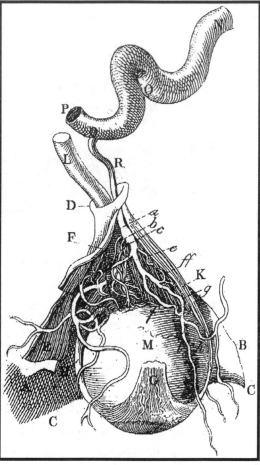

One day I came in to find the kids leaning over the map, all looking at the same spot, sounding as if they were competing for first place in a sports announcer's school. "There he goes across Turkey. He is now entering Iraq... No! He has turned North. He is entering Iran and making his way across to... No, he has jumped into the Persian Gulf and is entering Saudi Arabia...." They were following a bug across the world map. I thought it was a most effective homeschool method.

But last week we came to dinner to find the geographical maps replaced with thirteen full color posters of the human body. Now the Bible says that "no man ever yet hated his own flesh; but nourisheth and cherisheth it." I guess my wife thought there was no better place to observe the flesh than where we nourish it.

The boys quickly grew tired of observing the urinary tract during meal times. One afternoon, while eating a snack, I sat down where the boys usually sit and found I wasn't so hungry after two minutes of observing a bladder blockage. So I moved over one seat and tried to eat a bologna sandwich while looking at a dissection of the liver. The next meal I moved around to the girls' side and studied stomach and colon cancers until I developed indigestion. I finally tried my wife's seat and studied the brain until I felt I needed a lobotomy. My position at the end of the table is graced by a ten inch eyeball, complete with all the vessels and muscles. It reminds me of a Vietnamese dish I once ate. Did you know that the Superior Rectus muscle on the top and the Inferior Rectus muscle on the bottom enables your eye to look up and down? You didn't? Then how in the world can you read this newsletter?

I have studied the eyeball until I feel the whole body is an eye. But I moved to the opposite end of the table and found the answer to that verse of Scripture which asks, "If the whole body were an eye where were the hearing?" Simple. It's at the other end of the table. We are trying to find where my wife hid the world maps. ☺

Dear Mike and Debi,

Our pastor and his wife gave us a copy of your book and we can't describe the amount of peace it has brought into our home. We now have quick obedient children, and we now switch only about once a day. It's amazing that no matter who gets it, the others are careful in their actions also. We have used a rod (wooden spoon or switching stick) for a few years now, but never realized how much training we missed out on. Our love and fellowship with them has greatly increased. The anger and frustration that was once in our home is gone now. Our marriage has started improving also. We have gone through some struggles with self-denial and self-discipline, and the book has helped immensely on convictions in this area to be better examples to our children.

A Mother

The Selfishness of a Tender Heart

Y ou remember the many "Johnnys" in our book. His reputation was further confirmed as he came to visit us this week. As kids are apt to do, he quickly discovered a baby stroller—just made for a six-year-old with a gullible sister willing to act as the motor. With Johnny all laid back like Pharaoh, his sister powered the royal conveyance, visited every corner several times, and bumped every piece of furniture thirteen times. Becoming bored with the now familiar surroundings, he decided to direct his pilgrimage into the "forbidden room." The occupant of that room was lost in her meditation, but not so deeply as to fail to hear him command his chauffeur to push him into the occupied bedroom. Not wanting her furniture banged up or her solitude interrupted, the occupant commanded, "No, keep the stroller in the main room." Johnny, quietly—but not quietly enough—told his little sister to push him into the forbidden room anyway. I suppose Johnny thought he could always claim to be the helpless passenger of a stroller driven by his sister. Little sister was leaning into her burden and grunting too loudly to hear the "do not enter" command. As Johnny made his grand entrance, all laid back in his rickshaw, the mediator sprang from her repose and rushed to intercept the interloper. Just as she stood towering over the trembling intruder, his mother walked in, quickly appraising the scene.

Unfortunately for Johnny, his mama was having an emotional day. She was expecting a new baby and her heart, which is tender when she is at her toughest, was nothing but mush this day. You notice I said "unfortunately," because in order for Johnny to develop integrity, his mother needs guts. One look into Johnny's face assured her that he was under investigation for some alleged offense. "What's going on here?" Mama asked. The meditator calmly recounted the events. Johnny, realizing the finger of incrimination was pointing his direction, turned to Mama with an expression of innocent wonder and sincere confusion. Seeing that sweet little face, Mama knew that any accusation against him was false. She quickly began explaining that Johnny had hearing problems. She gave

Johnny the lie he needed. With hope in her gentle voice, Mama asked a question that assumed the answer: "You didn't hear her tell you not to come in, did you?" Now Johnny is old enough to have a master's degree in abnormal psychology (It only takes six years), so he immediately grasped the reprieve that his distraught mother had offered. But looking back at the towering, now censuring meditator, he was smart enough not to risk perjury. So he answered, "I don't know, I think I didn't hear her." Sound familiar? He doesn't want to be a liar, but it is so convenient.

Well, it was apparent that he had pleased Mama with his answer and relieved her of the pain. Mama knew Johnny was guilty, but something inside her wanted to protect her son at any cost; and the cost of making Mama feel better is often very high. Johnny was taught how to be a successful liar and manipulator. He also learned that telling lies makes Mama feel better. She would be angry if he told the truth, and it was obvious to him that she did not want the truth, so why be a fool and stick your head in a noose? Mama and son were accomplices in deception.

This mother had avoided facing her deception by a feeling that she was satisfying a deeper need to protect her little Johnny. But it was actually her own feelings she was protecting. Immediate, good feelings overrode her better judgment. If she were allowed to make a clear choice apart from emotion, she would do what is best for her son. But like an alcoholic, she is addicted to her "tenderness."

The verse that is the basis of the title of this newsletter is III John 4: *"I have no greater joy than to hear that my children walk in truth."* Parents, when you make it convenient for your children to be deceptive, you are leading them down paths of darkness. Bring your children to the light of truth. Value their honesty above all. I would take an honest scoundrel over a smooth, lying lover any day.

This story didn't end when the mother hastily rushed her children out of the house, away from the incriminating stare of the meditator now become denunciator. The next day she called with a broken heart. She is a devoted mother who truly desires what is best for her children. When she had time to get out from under the pressure of her feelings, she judged justly.

It is not too late for Johnny to break the lying habit, but when you wait until they are six-years-old to institute integrity, you have ingrained a character flaw that they will have to struggle against the rest of their lives. It is never too late to repent, but if we train them right, there will be areas in which they will never need to repent. It is better to train your children so that their energies can be applied to creatively serving God rather that struggling with their own weaknesses. One who spends his whole life trying to keep his head above water will never be involved in saving others. We want our children to be moral doctors not moral patients. Get tough, Mama.☺

Dear Michael and Debi,

Until I read this book I never realized how my beliefs had been undermined by what the secular "experts" say. My husband and I prayed about the information set forth in the book and we agreed to try it. It made a world of difference.

Our almost two-year-old son is very strong-willed. He has more freedom to explore and learn when his behavior is under control. We noticed improvement the same day we started the technique of switching as training rather than punishment. He needed a few days of adjustment before he understood fully and accepted the new routine. He has also become more affectionate with both of us. He was never the type to initiate kisses and hugs, but now it is pretty regular that he expresses affection. Maybe the training helps the child to be less focused on self and willfulness, and so they have the freedom to learn about things around them and the people around them.

I used the concept of training to stop him from crying so much. He wouldn't use the words he knew to get what he needed. So I consistently went through the same routine each time to demonstrate the language he needed to use. I didn't even have to switch him. He went through an explosion in his language shortly after this. The suggestions that the authors make in this book have helped to simplify my training with my son and have helped me gain better control over my anger.

M. H. from VA

Uncommon Common Sense

R ecently I asked two old-timers (men who remember seeing the first airplane or automobile that came to town, men that go to sleep before they finish telling the story) about how they would raise children. Their answers were accurate and would provide material for a new book. These old men, grumbling their views, are largely ignored. If they were thirty years younger, had a degree in child psychology from a "Christian" university and could speak with social grace, their statements would be received as profound. Packaged differently, their message would be highly acclaimed among today's parents.

When we stand before a crowd of eager parents and share the simple principles of parenting, we never cease to be amazed at their deep appreciation for simple truths. Concepts, that in former generations were common knowledge, are lost to today's parents. The mid-to-late twentieth century breakdown in discipline and family is not due to an inferior strain of children—nor to a corrupt society. Children are the product of their parents. Or to put it another way: To-day's children are a product of yesterday's children. Parents are children who grew up to have children. There is usually less than ten years between the child's last spanking and the first time he spanks his own child. Do years alone make one wise and bring maturity? Does the selfish, angry twelve-year-old mutate into a capable child trainer in the ten years before inheriting the job? The question we need to ask is, "What kind of parent is my child going to make?"

Why do some young people make good parents and others make lousy parents? The bottom line is that parenting skills are passed down from generation to generation. It is not necessarily a conscious effort. Most parenting techniques are never premeditated. When Deb and I began our family, we just took parenting for granted—as do most. We were both blessed to have had good parents of the old school. When we casually related to our children as our parents had related to us, we were usually doing the right thing. When we had a problem arise with one of our children, we usually found the answer in our own past experiences as children. By the time most parents have had enough experience to appreciate the issues and make adjustments, their children are already parents. Parents can mature and repent of their mistakes, but meanwhile their children are passing the same mistakes on to the grandchildren.

Western culture is in the midst of a cycle of degenerating family structure. Parents with young children must reverse this destructive trend while their children are still young enough to be programmed.

The way farmers used to get new chickens was to allow the hen to sit on her eggs until they hatched. The proud mother would lead the little chicks around the barnyard, teaching them what it meant to be a chicken. But unknowingly she was teaching them how to be good mothers when they grew up. When they grow up and are capable, they too will find a nice place to lay a dozen eggs and incubate them into chicks. Then, just like their mom, they will proudly carry on the farm tradition.

But there is a new way. Every spring, we go to the Co-op and buy a new batch of chicks. They have been hatched in an incubator and are only a few days old. When you look down in their box you notice that they are all grouped according to age and size, and usually grouped according to sex. They grow up with their peers. They remind me of children in a schoolyard or grouped in a daycare center. They learn to compete and survive in this prefabricated social order. It is not like the old barnyard, where the chicks followed the mother hen around looking for something to eat. The new way is much more efficient. Where efficiency is the goal, it is definitely progress. It is a fast new world, you know.

The only problem with this new way is that the young chicks, who grow up among their peers without a mother's care, have lost the natural instinct to be mothers. It is rare that one of these modern egg layers will devote the time and energy to sit on their eggs and care for young chicks. They are too busy with their own fulfillment to care for the brood of young chicks.

There are millions of young couples struggling to raise their brood, but somewhere in the former generations the knowledge of the simple "how to" was lost. For many of you raised in a classroom and nursed on TV, being a parent does not come naturally. You must imagine what parents should be like.

There seems to be a great awakening of families longing to raise a godly generation. It is a glorious sight traveling from place to place meeting hundreds of parents willing to hear and obey God's direction in raising a family. If you can just understand how you got where you are, you can better plot your journey back. You do not have ten years to recover what has been lost. Your children must be raised on right example. You alone are in a position to reverse this trend. The responsibility, with God's help, is yours alone. Today is the first day of the remainder of your child's life. Make it count. ☺

Heretic, Heretic!

I recently read an article in Readers Digest that affirmed what we already supposed to be true, that a child's IQ can be raised by early stimulation. By making eye contact with your infants and provoking them through all their senses, they get sharper intellectually. We have one perfect example here in our community. Caroline is not quite two years old and she is everybody's sweetheart. Since birth she has been constantly entertained by sixty kids and twenty-five adults.

Someone is always provoking her to repeat something. She is bilingual, sings any song, quotes Bible verses, speaks in paragraphs, and remembers everyone's name.

Last night we were having a special Bible study to tape messages on the book of Romans. Normally in our Bible studies, everyone participates and there is a lot of noise. On this occasion, all was supposed to be quiet. I had put in much preparation, hoping to produce a good quality tape for reproduction and distribution. Right in the middle of side one, during a most serious moment, I was mimicking a supposed objection. I said, "Do I hear a cry of heretic, heretic?" Following was a dramatic pause, in which we heard a wee, but yelled response of, *"heretic! heretic!"* Caroline has added to her list of 5000 vocabulary words. The response of the congregation was not so wee. I warned her parents: when attending other services, put a muffler on Caroline. Some places, such a cry would be too appropriate to be funny. ☺

Dear Mike and Deb,

I'm trying very hard to train at home so that I don't have to train in public. I've never before heard anyone address this and it just makes soooo much sense! Also, want to thank Debi for making the home schooling tape. It has given me so much freedom and has taken a ton of pressure off. I've been praying for a year now for God to prepare me to homeschool my son. I firmly believe that this was His answer for me.

TR from TX

Broken Insides   *By Debi Pearl*

S ome time ago, we were invited to speak to a small group. When we drove up, it was obvious they were a very conservative bunch, modestly dressed, and every family with a large, solemn following of children. As we piled out of the car and started unloading, there was a certain air of quiet foreboding over the place. Being a person with more than my share of imagination, I put my feelings down and entered with a smile. Mike seemed to be struggling as he spoke; I began to pray for him in earnest. At the close of the meeting, we were all tired and anxious to leave. The car was silent as we traveled down the dark, unfamiliar highway. Finally from the back, one of our young daughters spoke up, "All those folks seemed like their insides were all broken up." Poor grammar, but an excellent way to describe the people. The women all wore long dresses, and the men were dressed plainly, but it was like they were dead ancestors wandering back from an unwelcomed life of hardship. It was like they were mechanically programmed to say the right thing and look the right way. But there was no light in their eyes.

Over the next few days, Mike mentioned a couple of the men saying that years earlier God had called them to missions, but they couldn't find a mission board to take them. "Yes," I told him, "three different women told me that God had spoken to their husbands concerning missions early in their marriage, but they got so caught up in babies and making ends meet that they didn't pursue it." Two of our older children heard us talking and began relaying similar stories some of the people had told them. As this information began to take hold of our minds we fell silent with a contemplative brooding. My mind drifted back to the sober, tired, care-weary faces we met that night, and I silently bowed my head, "God save us from having broken insides." ☺

Dear Bro. and Sister Pearl,

   I want to say how thankful I am for your example of child training. It seems almost revolutionary, yet it's also so obvious and logical. How could Christians have been missing it for so long?   T&D

After Its Kind, and then some

W hen I see orange, the same shade as the fruit, I experience an involuntary citrus constriction in my jaw muscles. Likewise, when Autumn breezes bring the smell of hickory-wood smoke, it makes me feel good all over. On the other hand, when I see a chalk board, I feel pained and anxious. I know I am going to be called forward to write my spelling words for the entire third-grade class. These involuntary responses are the result of prior conditioning.

I recently received a letter from a mother who told of her little girl's conditioning to potty when she hears the sound made by a certain crib toy. The mother does not know how it happened, but somehow the child came to associate the sound of the toy with the release of her bladder. (I think she said the child was six months old.) The mother is now trying to use this happenstance conditioning to induce the child to go on the potty instead of in her crib.

Where smaller children are concerned, conditioning is a powerful tool. It can work both ways. All children are conditioned to respond to stimuli. It is inevitable. I have been in homes where the children went joyously nuts upon hearing Daddy driving up at the end of his work day. Later in life, without knowing why, they will still experience a leap of the heart when a car pulls into the driveway. Children, dreading the sound of a car bringing home an abusive father, will grow up to feel anxious at the sound of a car in the driveway.

When parents make it a habit to pacify their emotionally disturbed or bored children with a pacifier, the children grow up learning to cope by enacting the sucking motion. When they get a little older, they are pacified by having a cracker or sucker stuck in their mouths. Parents purchase peace by teaching their children to indulge their lusts to satisfy their feelings. Rather than learn self-control, they are channeled into lack of control. The children are thus conditioned to resort to eating as the answer to all stress, anxiety, and boredom. In other words, they are conditioned to eat. This not only generates lack of self-control in eating but produces a general approach to life that is one of indulgence and intemperance. The first sin of Adam and Eve involved putting something in their mouths. Christ's first temptation was an inducement to provide bread for his hunger. The mouth is the central focus of the lust of the flesh.

Your child is not evil in his desire to indulge, anymore than a dog is evil when he eats meat until he regurgitates. But dogs never grow into moral duty, as do children. Their reason never develops to the point of holding values higher than the instinct for survival and bodily pleasure. The child is designed to become more than a mammal seeking survival. The animal takes and devours with no thought to the needs of others. Children are destined by their Creator to mature to a plane of understanding and commitment wherein the passions are voluntarily subjected to the higher principles of the mind. It takes moral maturity to ignore even strong appetites and passions in favor of values deemed to be of more worth than gratification. To voluntarily lay aside one's gratification for the blessing and benefit of others is humanity at its finest. Indeed, true humanity is not found at the table, but at the altar—laying down one's rights and pleasures for love of others. God created us to be givers, not takers. The more costly the giving, the higher the humanity. The stronger the passion resisted, the deeper the soul of the man. Humanity increases in proportion to the difference between the strength of the pull of the flesh and the strength of soul to resist pure animal indulgence.

The end of the struggle between the flesh and the spirit is character—be it good or bad. History has revealed that all have fallen short of living up to his or her own aspirations to overcome selfish, bodily indulgences. There is nothing glorious about humanity indulging. The Bible says, "For all have sinned and come short of the glory of God (Rom. 3:23)." Certainly the sinfulness of man is clearly revealed in our willingness to indulge on the animal level. It is an ugly sight to see a parent ignoring, or even promoting, the child's indulgence. The cute, curly-headed, little darling grows into a puffy, pouting, flesh-parading, pile of inhumanity.

Parent, only you can save your children from that early conditioning toward unrestrained indulgence. We will not be able to condition them into being saints, but we can certainly condition them to sufficient self-control and self-respect that when the time comes, they will be more responsive to the call of God to repentance and faith.

The adult, when sufficiently motivated, can lean on his intelligence or his sense of values and override his early conditioning, but the child is not so developed in reason and self-reflection as to be able to make a decision purely on the basis of what he ought to do. The sluggard, the glutton, the thief, and the sexual pervert, to name a few, are children who grew up to have an adult's capacity for indulgence while retaining the child's lack of self-restraint.

When your children are only days old, begin watching for signs of their seeking to manipulate their environment to their gratification. At that age, all needs and desires are legitimate. But after several months they will learn ways to manipulate their cnvironment to not only meet needs but wants as well. They will need to be fed, but they also need to learn to wait. They need to bc held and cuddled, but you should not allow the child to always dictate the time and place. They will need attention, but they should not be allowed to grow up thinking that they can command the center of attention. Children will be more secure if you condition them to be patient and exercise self-control. Cause them to learn the meaning of the word *wait*. They should be able to accept a "No" without complaint. If you tell them "No," and they whine, they are already manipulating you to their own gratification. You have allowed negative conditioning. A child should be taught to sit where placed, lie down and be quiet upon command, and eat the food they are offered. To allow children to do only what they want to do is to cultivate the animal and to starve the human development.

I do not intend this to justify the hard, overriding, autocratic rule of some parents. Our job as parents is not to bear down with an autocratic spirit. We are not breaking a bad dog; we are nurturing a tender, developing plant. If you become nervous, anxious, and irritable, you will damage the delicate fruit. Children must be handled with kind, patient, loving hands.

As a parent—as an adult—you are still possessed of the natural passions and appetites that began even before birth. Your flesh lusts against your spirit. You know what you should do. Conscience speaks with a voice louder than our excuses. You may blame your parents for the bad programming. And they may well be the initial cause of some of your hang-ups. But you are now possessed of a mind and a spirit that is much the superior of your passions. Different from a child, you can choose to not yield to your weaknesses. Love of food, alcohol, and tobacco, or vanity of possessions, or bitterness of spirit may be more important to you than right doing, but you are absolutely free and able to step away from your early conditioning.

If a long history of self-will and indulgence has left your soul callused and your will weakened, you may say with the Apostle Paul, "for to will is present with me, but how to perform that which is good I find not (Rom. 7:18)." As an adult, you are not to blame for your moral weaknesses, but you are to blame for giving in to them. Moral helplessness is unwillingness of desire, not inability of faculties. If your children are to rise above selfishness, you must show them the way.

If you are a born-again Christian, you have been freed from all that you were in the old self. When Christ died, you died with him (Rom. 6:1-14). By faith you are now free from sin. You are no longer the "old man" conditioned to indulge. You are a new creature (2 Cor. 5:17), old things are passed away, all things are new. If you walk after the Spirit, you will not live after your lusts (Gal. 5:16).

In conclusion, if you walk after your lusts, it is because you choose to, but your children have no choice. Until they are old enough to know good from evil (Deut. 1:39), your responsibility is to function as your children's conscience and will. You must determine to train and condition them to a life of self-control and temperance. If you wait until they are old enough to understand their duty, they will already have a history of being totally given over to the flesh. Condition them now to be self-controlled and temperate in all things, and they will not bring into their Christian life a whole mess of twisted responses against which they must struggle. Parent, repent and lay hold of the freedom that is yours in Christ. Give your children a better start than you had. You are their only hope. ☺

Debi,

Last week the 11-year-old reminded 'mom' that a 'training session' would answer the problem of the 1-year-old's adventurous fascination with the stairs and not stopping at the 1ˢᵗ landing! Yes! It works on our "grands" too.

AB

See, I'm Happy Now

This past week there was another development in the ongoing saga of the Caroline files. Since she interrupted one of our Bible studies with an inappropriate announcement of "Heretic heretic," she has turned two years old and is increasing in much needed discernment. The other night some of the saints were visiting her parents when, in discontentment, she started whining. Her mother said, "Caroline, you be happy and stop whining." As Caroline continued to whine in an attempt to gain control of her mother, she was taken out and lightly spanked. A few minuets after returning to the room she again sought to establish her supremacy over her mother by whining and complaining. She wanted the attention being given to the visiting adults. Again she was spanked and told to be happy. When the mother returned her to their company, Caroline sat quietly for a few minutes and then, in the German Dutch language of the Amish, announced to all, "See, Mother, I am happy now." And she verified it with a big, sincere smile. Children who lead the family, do so with a miserable frown. Children that are forced to be in subjection will display a contented smile. Establish your authority and make your kids secure and happy. ☺

One for the Money

W hen we travel, teaching seminars, Deb and I enjoy observing many different families, each with its own unique personality. The personality of a family is as distinct as that of an individual. The parent who has the most influence in the home cultivates the family into his/her image. Some families are joyous and enthusiastic, while others are somber and stern. Some are thin skinned, quick to take offense with those inside or outside the family circle, while others are confident and secure, enjoying a continual by-play, never having their feelings hurt, believing the best of every situation. Some feel that the path through life is one of struggle and suffering, while others sing their way through.

This past week in Texas, we renewed acquaintance with a family we met about a year ago. The father is tall and angular. His crew-cut hair reveals a bony head reflecting nearly as much light as his face. It would take a plastic surgeon to remove his smile, and then there wouldn't be anything left but his muscular neck. His wife is equally joyous. She seems to be having a lot of fun being a wife and parent. They appear to be below any income bracket, and couldn't care less. The wife spoke with me when he was not around. She was proud of her man. Their children were animated.

They told several tales about how they dealt with problems that had arisen between the children. Their solutions were so creative, I wished I had thought of them first. Their little girl (I think they said four years old) was terribly afraid of the roaches sharing their humble dwelling. She would scream and try to flee, only to run into a creepy creature on the other end of the house. No amount of encouragement could relieve her of fear, but the father's sense of humor and creativity prevailed. He conceived of a way to rid the home of roaches, at less cost and danger than by an exterminator, and to occupy his energetic boys. He simply put a bounty on the roaches. The boys' hunter instincts, coupled with a touch of the entrepreneur, turned them into crawling safari men.

As the roach population diminished, the boys were becoming independently wealthy. After all, the wealth of a country, or home, is its natural resources. Day after day, the little sister stood quietly watching the boys counting their pennies and bragging about their exploits. The stack of pennies grew higher and higher, yet there seemed to be no end to the terrible creatures. Then one day, watching the boys line their dead roaches up and receive their reward, the little girl said, "Hang this, I'm catching roaches!" So the timid little girl who couldn't control her emotions gave the boys a run for their money as she scurried around under the furniture snatching up the crawling pennies.

The moral to this story is that self-control is a matter of sufficient motivation. ☺

Dear Deb,

Thank you so much for your articles "Carnal Husbands, Cranky Wives and Cantankerous Kids" and "Bound." Thank you for being straightforward and frank. I am grateful for older women like you who are teaching us younger women how to love our husbands and children the way God wants us to. You don't know how glad and sad I felt when I read them. Glad because I know God is leading me in His good and perfect way, sad because through your articles I saw that I am a critical wife and that I am binding my husband through my words, attitudes and actions. This is hard to admit, because I hate to be wrong. Lately I have been working hard to not get angry at my husband, and I can see that there is a change in him when I am at peace. Not only him, but just the atmosphere of our home.

A grateful wife in Michigan.
T. O.

On Close Examination

W hen you have spent ten minutes with a parent and child, you can feel whether or not there is a healthy environment for growth and development. Now we are not looking at how much they know or even how informed they are in parenting skills. To be able to define technique and principle is useful and often saves a lot of time when faced with a problem, but there is something that runs much deeper—as deep as the soul. We see parents who are socially clumsy, intellectually slow, and couldn't discuss child training with any coherence at all; yet they are good parents, raising stable, contented kids.

On the other hand, we know of parents that are wise enough to provide stimulating and challenging conversation on points of child training, parents that could probably teach an impressive class on the subject. They have read several good books, retained most of what they read, and are very confident of their abilities. Yet, as you see them relate to their children, you know they have problems that will bring disappointment to the home.

What is the missing element? It is a matter of the soul. We are not talking about religious indoctrination or spiritual airs; we are talking about the life and attitude that makes us who we are inside. In some homes you can sense that the parents and the children are just coexisting. By "chance" of nature they are sharing the same dwelling. They may maintain a compromising truce, bringing relative stability, but you can feel, if not see, their souls in competition. The parents have disciplined the children into subjection, but the children are not walking in their parents' light; they are walking around their parents' displeasure. There is no mutual respect and appreciation. Parents and children are walking separate paths. Due to the necessity of circumstances, their paths are running parallel, but they are not walking together, not in fellowship. They are all survivors of their corporate, social tension. For practical purposes they have learned to get along with various degrees of give and take.

Then there are those relationships where parents seem to have, as it were, invisible radio links to their children. It is like they were in constant communication. You sense that the parents' most important moment-by-moment task is to nurture their children. We are not talking about constantly indulging, or even constant attention, but just an awareness of their child's soul. The parents are ever on guard, stimulating, challenging, teasing, encouraging, appreciating their children.

If you were to approach a child who is part of such a culturing relationship and ask, "What does your mother/father think about you? The child would unhesitatingly, and with a contented smile, tell you, "My mama/daddy thinks I am great." I am by no means suggesting it, but if you were to teasingly say, "You are so much trouble, your mother is going to give you away." The child would not be angry. He/she would pity your ignorance or stupidity, condescendingly smiling at you as if to say, "Poor ignorant man. Doesn't he know that my mama would be unhappy without me?" How would your children answer if someone asked them how you felt about them?

Children who are tolerated and pacified feel insecure. They are angry. They come to such a frame of mind that if you told them their parents had decided to give them away, they would explode in anger, because they feel it could be true.

Only parents who feel desperate will admit to this condition. Many Christian homes are in this deplorable state. Busy, career-absorbed parents speed along through life, take their children to church, send them to youth camp, go to an occasional ball game, take them to Disney World, restrict the kids' TV, ration the sweets, make sure they get a good education, spank them when they are young, and nag them when they get older. They watch them go through all the "stages," and then one day the parents stop long enough to exclaim, "That ungrateful kid! I gave him/her everything. Why is he/she so angry? You would think I was the enemy! Oh well, it is out of my hands now. I just hope they don't bring that bratty grand-baby over here again this weekend."

If you fear you have allowed this condition to develop in your home, what can you do? You must change your entire philosophy of life. Your perspective and values must be revamped. Decide where your priorities lie. The key is to determine where you are going to invest your best emotional energy. When you can look in your child's face and smile with genuine relaxed pleasure and delight, you have turned the corner to renewal. When you can get in touch with your child's soul and know that your hearts are beating together, you have conquered. To maintain that fellowship is the best of parenting, and the best of what this life can offer.

Children are not deceived. They are great psychologists. They want to be loved, valued, appreciated, understood. Your conversion must reach all the way to the deepest recesses of your soul, or they will know you are fake.

John the Baptist, the forerunner of Christ, was given the ministry of preparing the nation of Israel for the coming of Messiah. His calling was "to turn the hearts of the fathers to the children, and the disobedient to the wisdom of the just; to make ready a people prepared for the Lord (Luke 1:17)." Fathers, mothers also, your children need your heart. There is no substitute, no technique, no wisdom, no program that can take the place of the heart. Your intelligence and education alone are worthless. Psychology is a deceptive vanity. Techniques, including the ones we teach, are paint brushes without artists. God breathed into us a living soul, making creatures with whom He can fellowship. If you would fellowship with your children, you must breathe your soul into them.

You may need to make adjustments that allow you to have more relaxed time with the children. But sometimes the problem is deep in the soul of the parents. If you cannot be heart-to-heart with your children, because your heart is corrupt, you need to go to God in repentance. When you have peace with God, you will exude peace in the home. You will become approachable to your children. They will come to enjoy just spending time with you. You will become their best friend. ☺

A Whole Boy

By Debi Pearl

As I look at the woman sitting opposite me, the twisting of her hands, the set of her shoulders, and the stress on her face tells me she is willing to do anything I suggest—another desperate parent; I shudder at the memories. The responsibility of knowing that what I say could make or break her child is more than I care to bear. Yet, here I am searching my mind for an answer, silently begging God to please tell me what to say. Letters are so much easier. There is time to think, to pray, to finally give up and throw the letter away. But now she waits, and I see her pain. Her son is eight years old. The professional diagnosis was Attention Deficit Disorder. He is angry, often explosive, and sleeps very little. His violence is usually directed at his brothers and sisters, but occasionally at his parents as well. His eating habits are not good. On occasion he wildly explodes, using vile curse words. The list goes on and on.

I know she loves him. I can see it in the twisting of her hands. But I can also see she doesn't like him. It is revealed in the frustration and bitterness of her voice. What one thing can I tell her? She asks about herbs to replace the drug he is taking. But neither drugs nor herbs are the answer.

I think about diet. I see the boy eating cheesy puffs and drinking coke. I know the yellow and red dye in the cheesy puffs has been found to contribute to his "problem."

My thoughts of diet are interrupted by the mother speaking of her past—and her husband's past. Yellow dye seems so unimportant now. They have surely given place to the devil. They carry the shadow of guilt. Their sins are past, but a sense of captivity remains.

I consider telling her of spiritual strongholds.

But before I speak she turns the conversation to homeschooling and I see and hear the tension increase. "He refuses to sit still. He constantly bothers the other children. It is a nightmare trying to get him to do his work." Again I start to answer, "He doesn't need to sit still," but I realize this isn't the answer either.

Quickly and without even knowing, she turns the conversation again, this time to sickness, "He's on antibiotics again this month," she replies offhandedly. My ears perk up and I want to jump on my favorite bandwagon, but still I know there's more. She begins to wind down when she starts talking about child training, our book, lack of early discipline, baby-sitters, public school, anger in the home, TV, etc.

She wants me to tell her some singular thing to *do* that will make it all right. Her child is a complex singular being, but the roots run out in all directions. He has a body that is reacting to antibiotics, red and yellow dyes, sugar, lack of self-discipline, and lack of sleep. He has emotions that are being bottled up in an unnatural school structure. He has a spirit that is being tortured by the devil who lurks about seeking whom he may devour. He has a mind that is being filled with the lust of Hollywood, the anger of his parents, the licentiousness of public school, the bitterness of his baby-sitter, and more. He is a whole boy whose body is being poisoned, his mind filled with ugliness; his soul is being destroyed, and his emotions are going wild. You can drug his body, numbing the vehicle of his soul, but someday he has to be freed from those drugs, and when he is, the sickness of his soul will again be revealed.

Looking into the eyes of this hurting young mother, I wish with all my soul I could give her the quick fix she so urgently desires, but there's not one answer. The child's problems are many and complex. It would take a book, and still all the answers would not be found.

Clean. He needs to be made clean. He needs a clean body, free of poisons, sugars, and dyes. He needs a clean home, free of anger, Hollywood, and deceit. He needs a clean day, free to roam the countryside until his body is relaxed and tired. He needs a soul cleansing that can only be found in Jesus and His shed blood. He needs a clean daddy whose heart wants only to bring healing to his son. He needs a clean mother, whose heart is turned to honoring and reverencing her husband. He needs a clean world, both physically and spiritually. This little boy has big problems. He is bearing the penalty of a generation of neglect.

How do I tell his mother? Where does she start? After listening to the whole story I finally know. It must start with her, for she is the one seeking a solution. This mother can't clean up the world. She can't dictate to daddy; that would create further strife. But she can decide to honor and reverence her husband, thus bringing to her son at least one area of peace and security. She can go to the library and study the effects of foods, dyes, and sugar, then take that information and act on it. She can take him to a place where he can run for hours, instead of forcing him to labor over a workbook that will never make a difference now or in eternity. She can pray, asking God for a miracle both in herself and her son. She can laugh and sing the joy of the Lord right into his presence. Everyday, he needs her smile. If she will do these things, it will be a beginning. Like a young tree bent in the wrong direction, she can begin to straighten that which is crooked.

If you identify with this mother's condition, right now ask God to forgive your rebellion toward your husband. Stop your grumbling and ask God to fill your soul with thanksgiving. Ask God to give you wisdom. He has promised wisdom to all those who ask. So ask and keep on asking, and go out looking for information to help your son. No one loves him like you do. No one has your willingness to do something about it. No one can help your son like you can. He needs your heart first, and then you need his. This whole boy needs a whole solution. ☺

Dear Michael and Debi,

I feel as if I owe you my life. There's no way I can describe the transformation which has taken place in our home. And it is getting better every day. My miracle baby was born after 7 years of marriage. I was 38 years old. What can I say? We spoiled her.

My husband and I both came from abusive homes and we were determined not to do to our child what had been done to us. We went too far the other way.... At age 8 he was mouthy, smart-alecky and had a terrible temper, etc. I read your books. I did as you said and applied the rod. It only took 1 1/2 weeks for the changes to stick. He's a changed kid inside and out! My husband is amazed. We are all so much happier. It is as if an angel has passed through our home.   JC

Rowdy Boys

Question: Do you have any
cures for rowdy boys during
school? It's almost always in fun,
but is always disruptive."

Yes, there is a very simple and
final solution. You just throw the
boys away and get all girls. This will
also end all wars and stop all competitive sports. I might add that the
termination of the male population
will likewise put a stop to great ar-
chitecture, canals dug thought the
swamps, irrigation projects, high-
ways through the mountains, and the
invention of machines that make life
easier.

I know mothers don't expect
their little boys to display male ag-
gression so early, but little boys are
just baby men. I know that young
boys don't have the wisdom and self-control to sensibly direct their
hormonally prompted drives. They are often rowdy and hyper. If
there could only be a drug that could make them act more sedate
like the lovely female population, or maybe a drug that would just
postpone their development…. But wait, I have heard that there is
such a drug. It is called Ritalin. The government, which is commit-
ted to a sexless society, is encouraging and promoting the use of this
and other drugs to subdue the young male population.

You gave birth to a boy; you will have to deal with him as such.
If you wanted something that purred and laid around the house, you
should have gotten a cat, not a boy.

God created the male race to work outdoors in a garden environment. Man's nature and role are to subdue. Each man needs his own
independent domain to conquer and dress. That's why we see so

many overworked yards in the subdivisions. Those tiny plots of buildings, grass, and shrubs are each man's Garden of Eden. With an assortment of steel tools, he conquers his resisting frontier. His incessant overworking of such a small kingdom reminds me of a tiger going out for a stroll in his twenty square foot cage, but stroll he must.

Most men are finding some form of expression and release in work and sex. But young boys placed in classrooms become like tiger cubs scolded for tumbling with their fellows. Such confinement and restriction is against nature. Have you noted the primary activity of any young animal? It is to playfully attack the members of his family. Boys are made to run, tumble, goad, and respond in kind. It is not natural for a boy to sit in a cage. If we put him in real bars, it would be easier for him, but to force him into confinement for lengthy periods is against his nature and is torturous indeed.

Homeschooling should not be an attempt to reproduce the classroom setting. The Bible defines the context in which we should teach our children. "And thou shalt teach them diligently unto thy children, and shalt talk of them when thou sittest in thine house, and when thou walkest by the way, and when thou liest down, and when thou risest up (Deuteronomy 6:7)." In other words, our teaching should be part of our ongoing daily activity, not a special event that demands long periods of withdrawal from the real world.

But our questioner is still waiting for a practical response to the question about how to prevent rowdy boys from disturbing the classroom setting. Provide release and expression for their boyishness, and do so with sufficient frequency and intensity so as to "decompress" them. That is, keep the classroom down to, say fifteen minutes, with work or hard play between times. If you feel you must have a longer time of instruction or practice, have them jump up and do 100 side-straddle-hops before they resume. Have them sing out a chant or count real loud as they exercise. You may have to study a military sergeant's manual. Provide a reward for the fastest ten laps around the house. Have them do their math while standing on one foot. Make them place their tablet on the wall and write while standing up. Keep them alert, interested, and exhausted. Don't try to contain and teach a tornado. Give it a time and place to expend its energy, and then teach when it is a little breeze. One hour of fun schooling is worth more than eight hours of drudgery. ☺

Sorry, I'm Tied Up Now

In keeping with our article on boys I have decided to relate an event that occurred last week. About twenty-five of us from the church, old and young, went camping and whitewater rafting. Deb and I didn't raft, but we did camp out and cook over the open fire. During the evening, one of the little seven-year-old boys named Asher buzzed around the camp in his cut off pants. He was to be my charge the next day when his daddy floated the river. He is a wiry looking rascal of a kid.

He had forgotten to bring along a belt, so his pants just rode on his hips, revealing four inches of his Fruit of the Loom. During the first hour, at least a dozen people had told him to pull his pants up. I took note that he made no effort and had actually begun to use it as a way of getting attention. So I took some cord and offered to make him a belt. To my surprise, he resisted. When I made mild forceful attempts to tie his pants up, his resistance intensified. Look out! He was getting out of the pecking order. So I forcefully held him down while I tied up his pants. When I turned him loose he immediately began to act like a boy/man. He expressed his independence and defiance by cheerfully, in a competitive manner, making an attempt to untie the cord. This was still all in fun, but as a man responsible for the upcoming male population, I treated him as I would one of my own boys. I gave him a stern (while laughing) warning, "If you untie that cord, I will get a longer piece and tie you up in a manner that will make you sorry." But he was determined to have it his way. I was determined that he should learn a little fear and respect (all in serious fun, mind you). He got the attention of the whole group as he finally freed himself. No backing up now. I couldn't allow this boy to grow up without respect for "the powers that be." So I obtained a fifteen-foot length of cord and chased him down. I weigh 230 pounds, and I am six feet, four inches tall. He is about four feet tall and weighs about fifty pounds. He put everything into his resistance, and I was thankful he wasn't half my size or I might have failed in my endeavor. I just knew he had six legs and seven arms. I had to sit on his head and shoulders to work the cord through the loops of his pants. He squirmed and kicked so that it felt like trying to contain a big coiled spring. Then I had to flip him over so I could thread the other side. He nearly got away that time. I was afraid he was going to bite me on the rear pocket. By this time we had a large cheering crowd. He was the favored contender. The encouragement only gave him strength. Between the flickering firelight, the flashing of cameras, the cloud of dust and the cheering, it must have looked like a real sporting event to the other campers.

To be true to my threat, after securing his pants, I ran the cord up over his shoulders, like suspenders, and down around his legs, drawn up like a calf, and finally tying one hand to his waist where his foot was tied. By his time I was laughing so hard that I could hardly continue; besides, I had used up the cord. But I had taught the little rebel his lesson: Don't fool with the big guys; you always lose. So I jumped up, intending to step back and admire my handy-work, but something was wrong with my feet. I nearly fell on my face. When I tried to catch my balance, I found I couldn't separate my feet. Here I was doing this duck walk across the camp, my body bent halfway over, reaching for the ground to ease my collision, when I realized that in all this struggle, the kid had tied my shoe-laces together. How he did it with me sitting on his head I will never know, but we learned our lessons. He kept the belt on, and I am going to pick on people more my own age and size. He is my kind of boy though.

I told you this story to define boys. I wouldn't have them any other way. While I was making an unsuccessful attempt to untie my shoelaces, which finally had to be cut, the father was laughing and bragging about his boy. He thinks his kids are the greatest. They all know it, and are intolerably proud, secure, and happy. He doesn't try to subdue them. He builds hurdles and teaches them to jump.

Our kids ought to be our favorite comedians, our most frequent pastime, our main hobby, our primary project, our best friends, our consuming passions, and the center around which all future plans revolve. That's child training. ☺

"Train up a child in the way he should go: and when he is old, he will not depart from it (Proverbs 22:6)."

Tying S~~trings~~ Bows

By Debi Pearl

Over the years, families develop patterns or habits. We were no exception. When Mike was yet unmarried, the church where he pastored gave him a huge brown recliner. When we married, the recliner was always given a place of honor in our house. It was called "Daddy's chair." Mike would come in after a long day of work and park his big body in the recliner to wait for supper. The children took that opportunity to minister to Daddy. One child would scratch his head while the other would take his shoes off and rub his feet. The youngest child would have the honored position in Daddy's lap, brushing his beard. It usually took Daddy only 2 minutes to fall asleep. The kids didn't mind; having Daddy asleep or awake was fine play.

It is amazing how creative children can be. By the time Daddy came to supper, he was either combed down slick, looking like an old tintype picture, or sticking out in all directions, looking like a wild pirate. Of course, he never knew nor cared how he looked after one of those sessions. He just enjoyed the time of being scratched, rubbed, combed, and adored by the children.

Now to understand and appreciate this story you need to know just a few more facts. Mike is a big man, reaching in his salad days to about 6'5" tall. His normal weight was about 220 or 230 lbs. His hair was full and dark, almost black, and his beard was full, bushy, long, and black. In my youthful over-zeal, I prided myself as being very frugal. Therefore his tee shirts were always one or two inches too short, due to the local Dollar Store not carrying X-large-X-tall sizes. I bought black tee shirts because they didn't show stains and could be worn as a shirt, thus further saving money spent on clothes. So now you have a clearer picture of Mike while the children were growing up. A huge man with a big black beard, with an inch of his mid-riff showing every time he moved. He had a habit of always pulling down his shirt. Now that he is an older, more distinguished man, I make myself pay extra for tee shirts that fit. But back then he was not yet so distinguished and I was very frugal.

Anyway, you get the picture.

One Saturday he had been working in the heat of the day. When he walked in the door, he collapsed in his chair and the kids rushed to minister to him. They brushed, combed, styled, rubbed and scratched; yet he continued to snore. In the midst of all this styling, creativity was born. Just a couple of days earlier, Nanny (grandmother) had given our youngest girl a large package of multi-colored, plastic, hair barrettes. While Daddy peacefully slept, the kids transformed their strong macho daddy into a cute, braided, dolled-up fellow. Still Daddy slept; so the children got tired of waiting for him to awaken and went to comb the dog. Later, when I heard him stirring around and knew he was awake, I called out from the kitchen and asked him to go to the store for a few items. So off he went. Yes, you guessed it, with pink, red, yellow, and purple bows and ribbons decorating his beard and hair. About an hour later he came walking in the door a humble man, still in complete ignorance of why people were staring and snickering at him. He had spent an embarrassing hour trying to figure out what was so funny. He had checked his pants first; no problem there. After noticing several more laughs, he checked the backside. No, they were solid. He then decided just to hold down his shirt, but still the giggles. Now, you must understand, people usually don't go around laughing at a man that big and hairy. Like I say, I hardly noticed the bows when he walked in, because he looked soooo humble. It is incredible how different a person looks who has just had a good humbling. Of course, then I noticed the rainbow of plastic girlie barrettes. When I couldn't control my laughter, he knew he had problems and headed for the bathroom to discover how he, Big Mike, could suddenly become a laughingstock. The mirror revealed the truth. Always a good sport, he had a good laugh as well.

For months he always headed to the mirror when the kids were through with him. Time passed and the children grew; his dignity returned. Ten years ago when we moved up here to the country, our youngest was 3 years old. Now there were only 2 little girls to groom Daddy, and with the passing of time, he forgot to check the mirror. When a man is young, people are not so surprised when he acts or dresses in a strange manner. Also, city people are generally a weirder lot. They are not often surprised when they see strange things. But in our rural community, people are usually quite conservative, if not downright backward. So when this large, middle-aged, plain looking man entered the grocery store with bows and barrettes of every color and shape holding his beard into several braids and his graying hair into standing knots, he was a spectacle so strange, so bizarre, and so ridiculous that the open mouthed stares and uncontrolled laughter immediately alerted him to a problem. Without even bothering to check his pants or hold down his shirt, he quickly left his grocery cart in the aisle and headed out the door. The car mirror confirmed his worse fears. He was indeed one of those "kind."

He has never completely recovered. Now when you invite him to do seminars, this dignified, gray-haired man will stand before you with a habit born of reinforced memories. With a distracted air he will run his hands over his hair a couple of times before he begins smoothing down his beard. We meet eyes and grin. He silently communicates, "Just checking, just checking." And I smile, silently communicating back, "Just you wait, before too many years there will be grandchildren and you've still got some hair." ☺

Dear Michael and Debi,

I have been reading Rebekah's Diary and have been touched by her honesty of feelings and thoughts and God's continual provision. It is so normal to be caught up in this world and its meaningless possessions and daily activities. We are born and trained to care so much about meaningless activities and things. It is probably honoring to God to take proper care of the things He has provided for us - but what about decorating and color coordinating and constantly wanting everything to be in its proper place and feeling so CRAZY when it is not! These things were so modeled for me as a child and it seems insurmountable to just throw these feelings out of my brain. I wish – I pray – that I could care only about honoring God – and not man! I find myself wanting to live longer so I can have time to get better in my life of attempting to honor God.

M. C., from N. C.

So, Who's Disabled?

"**M**other, why are you cleaning up this room; isn't this your little girl's room?"

"Yes, but she's only three, not big enough to clean up yet."

"Oh! And who took the toys out of the box and scattered them on the floor?"

"She did."

"So her ability to transport toys works in only one direction?"

"Mother, you look so tired. Why are you fretting so over the laundry, the dishes, the house cleaning, etc., when you have three children in there fighting over toys?"

"Oh, I will tend to them when I get the time."

"No, I mean, why don't you put them to doing some of these chores? Perhaps then they wouldn't be so bored, fussing and fighting all the time."

"Well, the oldest one is only seven, and it is more trouble trying to get them to work than it is to do it myself."

When they are two and three years old, it is more trouble to involve them than it is to do it yourself, but if you wait until they are actually big enough to be of real assistance, by then they will have developed routines and habits that do not include working. If you serve the children until they are three or four—maybe even six or eight—and then try to get them involved, they feel that you are making uncalled-for demands. If, on the other hand, you involve them in helping themselves and others from the time they are walking, chores will be natural to them. There will be no hassle, no unlearning process, no abrupt change in policy.

Some parents underestimate the potential of their children. Others feel guilty for demanding their children assume responsibility. By the time most parents decide their children are old enough to assist in the work load, they have already instilled in them the assurance that Mother is their servant and they are the deserving recipients. When Mother tries to reverse the "Mama is servant" trend, the kids will raise such a fuss about helping, that Mother retreats, finding it more comfortable to be a complaining servant than to trouble herself teaching them. To fail to teach the young ones responsibility simply because you detest conflict is to surrender to timidity as a vice.

Certainly, we do not want to demand more of our children than they are capable of giving, for that could be very discouraging to them. But to demand less than their capabilities is to permit a dispensation of irresponsibility and unnecessary dependence, which breeds weakness. Those who expect servitude are always unthankful. Those who receive servitude will come to demand it when it is withheld or delayed. Don't wait until you feel ridiculous serving big kids before you decide to place responsibility upon them.

Have you ever felt that your children fail to appreciate the things you do for them, that they take you for granted? It is your fault, not theirs. You have babied them, made them weak with your giving. You gave them everything, but what they need most is independence, self-sufficiency, skills, discipline, thankfulness, and the ability to serve others. If you serve children until you are confident they are fully capable of serving themselves, you have cultivated slothfulness in them. When you become critical of the way they fail to do their chores, it is a sure statement that you have waited too long to involve them. Why are you angry at them? You bent the tree, so it grew in the direction you pointed it.

Many parents actually serve their little ones by placing few demands on them. This builds dissatisfaction as the parents grow tired and overworked, wondering why the kids don't help out more. When they finally attempt to demand more from them, they are met with complaint and protest. Finally, selfish frustration is triggered; a frustration born out of criticism and the unavoidable sense that their children are domestic parasites.

Why do parents wait until their children's slothfulness is pervasive? Most parents are ruled by their own feelings. They don't have a preconceived plan for training their kids; they just wait until pressured and then REACT. When they grow tired of serving them or become irritated at their ineptitude, they are provoked to demand participation. The motivation to demand responsible participation from their children does not come about as the result of a conscious decision to train the children for their own welfare, but as a result of the parents' involuntary irritation.

You know that you have waited too long to turn over responsibility when doing so causes the children to rebel and feel mistreated. At this point, the children are resisting the new, invasive order. A confrontational spirit then arises between parents and children. The anxiousness and criticism of parents prevents them from being trainers. They are antagonists. At this late date in the child's life (five or six years old), parents are trying to fix something that is broken, rather than mold something that is growing.

If you unexpectedly gave your neighbor $1,000.00, he would be embarrassed to take it. After your urging, explaining that you are just making more than you need and thought that it would be a blessing, he would finally receive it with a profusion of thanks. When you again gave $1,000.00 the following week, he would receive it with less reluctance. After one year of receiving his weekly gift, he would receive it with a quick nod and a formal thanks. Then when you suddenly stop giving money to him, but instead give it to the man across the street, your original recipient would have his feelings hurt. He might even be angry. He would want an explanation. You see, after a year he would have adjusted his lifestyle to your gifts. He may be so dependent on your gift that he would be financially damaged when you stop giving. He has become your expectant dependent. Your gifts have weakened him. You would probably loose his friendship upon discontinuing the gifts. His bad attitude was created by your unnecessary benevolence.

Parents weaken their children by doing everything for them, by serving them, treating them as if they were handicapped. But then even handicapped children are not always treated so. I recently read an article in a little periodical called "NATHHAN News." It is a monthly publication dedicated to parents with *special needs* children. By permission, we reprint a condensed version of an article written by Tom and Sherry Bushnell, parents of 9 children, (3 adopted, 5 birth, and one about to be birthed). Three of their children have various physical and mental disorders. I believe they are greater experts in the field of dealing with handicapped children than any expert with initials after his name. We submit to you their years of experience and success. If a parent can raise a happy, obedient, hard working, emotionally well adjusted, Down syndrome, teenage son, then we parents with average children have no excuse.

TRAINING UP DISABLED CHILDREN

Written by Tom and Sherry Bushnell

Along with the knowledge of how to please God, we must teach ourselves and our children to be self-controlled. Here are some positive ways self-control will benefit our special needs children.

* Learning to obey quickly, regardless of whether they understand totally "why," will assure them more safety.

* Not pouting or whining when asked to do something adds to their capabilities. Practicing self-control helps our children avoid the habits of laziness, self-centeredness, and stubbornness.

* If we are diligent to teach our children self-control while they are young, when they are teens they will reap the positive benefit of being morally pure. Looking lustfully at the opposite gender, masturbation, or feeling sorry for one's self can be real difficulties with older special needs children.

Sometimes the things we ask our children to learn are very hard, physically or mentally. When our children are disabled, it takes much more effort not only to do tasks, but to have a good attitude while trying. Do you know that a child's habit of giving up when frustrated may be encouraged by us parents?

To pity our children because we feel guilty or sorry for them is a mistake. It may be almost as painful for us to watch our children fail again and again as it is for them to keep trying. For instance, our daughter with cerebral palsy and autism, age 5, has the use of one hand; that's it. Her feet stick straight out and her left arm is tucked into her chest. A while ago, she was really getting frustrated because she was the last one to be helped to get dressed. Every morning she would come down the stairs fuming, ready for a fight. Tired of her pouting, we decided that she needed to learn to get dressed herself. She was horrified. She spent the first 2 weeks getting to the breakfast table with only one arm in the same leg hole in her sweat pants.

Except for verbal encouragement and the initial lessons, we did not help her or allow her brothers or sisters to help her. After breakfast, she spent the rest of the morning on the living room carpet, finishing dressing. **We consistently disciplined her for anger and pouting, and strongly encouraged her to try harder, not allow-**

ing her to give up.

In reality, it was a lot of work for all of us. She knows just how to look totally helpless. She puts on her "I'm so sad" expression, aimlessly making half-hearted attempts at finding the right arm hole. From past observation, we knew she was simply waiting to see if there wasn't someone who would rescue her.

It was hard for her siblings to watch her try and not accomplish much. They pitied her. One of her brothers felt so sorry for her that when he knew we weren't looking he put her arm in the right hole. She was very grateful, but it didn't help her the next day when he wasn't around and she still had to find a way to accomplish the task herself. After 4 weeks, she was able to get dressed in about 4 minutes. Boy, was she excited! So were we.

Teaching our special needs children to hang in there and keep trying whole-heartedly will make them useful servants for our Lord. Children that force others to wait on them are more disabled for their vice.

It is a crippled heart that will render them morally and even physically unfruitful for the Lord, not a delayed mind, missing eyesight or hearing, short attention span, or poor memory.

Doing more for our children than we should creates tyrants. It takes a lot of work to teach our children self-help skills, but if they are at all bodily able (even if it takes them a long time) they should. **As adults, our** *special needs* **children will not be a social menace by constantly manipulating and imposing on others if we teach them perseverance and self-control now.**

What then is the answer to the title of this article: *So, Who's Disabled?* Parents, of course. Through their own weaknesses they have established lazy habits that their selfish kids will not allow them to break. You may say, "So, I know I messed up when they were young; is my fourteen-year-old too old to train into taking responsibility?" The question is: "Are they too old for you to have the courage to stand firm in demanding they be responsible?" It is the parents that need training.

The military inducts eighteen-year-old men, most with slothful habits. Can you imagine being responsible for fifty teenagers? No doubt, most of them walked out of a messy room when they left home. Mama will miss them but not the extra work they caused her. But in just a few days, one man has turned all fifty boys into very disciplined, neat, punctual, respectful men. How did he do it? Fear. He is bigger, tougher, and means every word he says. He is even serious when he lowers his eyebrows. He doesn't speak twice—may not speak once. You'd better guess what he expects, and make sure it is done in record time.

Now, Mother, you may not be tough enough to bring discipline into the life of your eighteen-year-old, but if you would take a double dose of a supplement known as *backbone iron*, you could. What about your ten-year-old? You can still strike fear in his heart, can't you? He doesn't have to be afraid of you beating him, just know you are standing firm on your word.

Let's hear it one more time: *"I work my hands to the bone and no one even cares. They lie around and let me do all the work."* You did a good job of training them. The fault is in your own cowardliness. When they were three or four, you took the easy road, since at that age it was not so humiliating serving them, and now you have a habit that you can't break. You depend on them to depend on you. They do their part, which is to consume without giving and without being thankful. And you do your part, which is to complain, gripe and serve.

Have you got the guts to go on strike? To quit? Mother, stand up and proclaim, *"Do it yourself or it won't get done. It won't get cooked, washed, picked up, cleaned, purchased. You won't go, eat, sleep here, or have a moment's peace until it is done right and on time. I will say no more. It's your move, kid."* Then smile and walk off with confidence, knowing you have gone as far as you are going to go. There is a new order, now and forever, come what may. Then the most important last step is absolute consistency on your part.

It's your move parent. If you are tough, your home will become a more cheerful place.

We would like to give special thanks to NATHHAN News, 5393 Alpine Rd. S.E., Olalla, WA 98359 and for allowing us to edit and reprint portions of this article found in their wonderful publication. If you are looking for good reading, order this periodical.☺

June Bug

Most of you live in cultures quite different from ours here in middle-Tennessee. One of the dear ladies in our church, widowed, 57 years old, lives alone, deep in the woods, on thirty-six acres. She just came to know the Lord this past summer through the witness of our good friend Tom Slayman. Her dwelling is an eight-foot travel trailer with no running water, electricity, or toilet facilities. I am not telling you this to make you feel sorry for her. She is as contented as a squirrel in a beech tree. She sometimes works here in the office and buzzes around like a bug. Her name is June, so I call her "June Bug."

Just the other day she came rushing into the house holding up a torn piece of paper that read "Happy Birthday." She insisted that I tell her who was responsible. Not me, I didn't even know it was her birthday. She told how she returned home to find that sign attached to a new, double-seater outhouse, which had suddenly appeared not too far from her trailer, complete with a freshly dug hole. What a blessing! No more whistling winds on cold nights. Privacy, just in case a hunter should get lost and wander too deep into the woods. Have you counted your blessings lately? You don't complain do you? June doesn't.

Now you may be wondering, as I am, what a widow would need with a two-seater. "It could be prophetic," I told her. She is not looking, but you never know—with a vacant seat. ☺

In Defense of Boys—Again

Dear Mr. Pearl

In the July issue of "No Greater Joy," you answered someone's question concerning curing rowdy boys during school. Your answer seemed to be basically not to try to discourage it, but rather channel it. I homeschool my eight-year-old and I agree with your advice in this situation. However, your answer left me a bit confused, because your advice in "To Train Up A Child" is to expect completed compliance from children. One example in particular I remember being given is that of behavior during worship. You were comparing a mother who was continually having to stop and correct misbehavior to a mother who had trained her children to sit attentively at home. I have been trying to follow this advice, but the article on rowdy boys caused some doubt in my mind. Can you help clear this up?

Thank you,

CC

Answer

Y ou are not alone. We have received several letters from confused readers. However, for every confused reader there were ten who found solace in knowing their boys didn't have a Hyper-Horrible disorder.

I didn't say that boys should be allowed to be disruptive or disrespectful in the classroom setting, but that due to their aggressive natures, they should not be made to endure long periods of inactivity. I quote my article Rowdy Boys: "Provide release and expression for their boyishness, and do so with sufficient frequency and intensity so as to "decompress" them. That is, keep the classroom down to fifteen minutes, with work or hard play between times." I did not mean to imply that boys should be allowed special dispensations of disobedience, that we should permit them to violate the rules. Rather, by understanding that they are different from girls, from men even, as teachers we should parcel out the times of concentration with intermittent periods of more physical expression.

Boys can be made to sit still for eight hours without squirming, but who wants to be the minister of suffering? Their learning curve goes down in proportion to the time they are made to be inactive. Our goal is not to test the strength of our discipline or the perseverance of your boys. We just want to educate them with the least amount of intrusion. Crushing and subduing childhood is not our goal. We want to channel their impulses and direct them to the most balanced and creative personal expressions.

I had sufficient control of my boys that I could have made them sit quietly in one spot until they dropped from exhaustion, but I never had anything to prove. When they stopped having fun, we did something else, we did it a different way, or we did it later.

The Chinese classroom is a noisy place. The children all read out loud together. If you will keep the home a fun place instead of a morgue or a concentration camp, the children's souls will be growing while their minds retain a few necessary facts.

So I repeat, we are not suggesting that boys go unrestrained, but that we make allowances for their penned up drives to occasionally explode. Provide the time and the place, and you won't have to try to continually cap Old Faithful. ☺

Dear M & D,

Thank you for your book. The difference in our home and our children's cooperation has been astounding. The most gratifying change has been in my own attitude. No longer do I try to avoid being with my children (a difficult thing to do when one is a homeschooling housewife!). I now gladly incorporate them into my chores and my leisure time.   *Mary*

The Challenge of Teaching

By Greg Stablein, coordinator of Gateway Christian Schools.

I had a good opportunity to teach my sons a relevant lesson about locks as I replaced the one in our front door. With an enthusiastic voice I said, "Boys, look here. Do you want to see how a lock works?" A nod or word of acknowledgment was their unenthusiastic reaction. What was wrong? There couldn't be a more practical, real, relevant opportunity to learn. When plan A didn't work, I didn't give the boys an F. I realized that the lesson hadn't been adequately presented. Instead of giving up, I groped for a better approach. After asking the LORD for help, I challenged them, "Which of you could take this lock assembly apart (including the tumblers and springs) and then reassemble it so that the same key would unlock it? The change was dramatic. ☺

In the beginning when there was a Theos but no theologian.

When the Logos had not yet spoken that which came to be written.

Before the papari were brought forth or the ancient scrolls unrolled.

God yet existed in a state that for deity was befitten.

Without the help of a Scholar or a man of clerical collar,

He spoke and it was done, He commanded and it stood fast.

He called no committee nor asked any advice,

Yet His word alone was able to suffice.

by Michael Pearl

Child Training Marathon

Deb and I were teaching several seminars in a one-hundred-mile radius. One family requested that we stay with them the entire week and critique their child training. It was a busy, trying time for them, preparing meals and hauling us around from town to town, with meetings every night and sometimes all day. On top of all that, they assured us of their desire that we be diligent to tell them any and every thing we saw in them or their children that could be improved. If an occasion arose and we didn't speak out, they brought it to our attention and asked how and what should be done. This family meant business.

When we arrived, we assumed they must be having problems with their teenagers, since parents usually don't panic until they have a teenager making their lives miserable, but that was not the case. By today's Christian standards, they had a well ordered home. Their oldest child, a boy of about seventeen, was a real joy to his parents. But as the children got younger, there was a definite deterioration in their attitude and self-control.

I am not sure why this is sometimes the case. Often parents seem to tire of the rigors of teaching and discipline and begin to slack off with their younger ones. Or perhaps when the older children are turning out all right, parents ease up on their vigilance, taking their success for granted. And then, family values often change as economic success interrupts family unity. And of course, when a marriage slowly erodes, the younger children will not be rooted in the same loving, secure environment, as were the first ones.

This family had applied the teaching of our first book, and saw great improvement. But their six-year-old boy occasionally went into a rage when things didn't go his way. He was a very good psychologist. When angry, he would express his hurt feelings in a way that caused the parents to feel guilt, evoking just enough doubt and insecurity to keep them from being tough. Being cautious to deal with his "touchy" emotional state, they resorted to pleading and reason, explaining how "they really did love him" and how "he was not a bad person."

I watched the boy commit an offense, throw a fit when corrected, and then end up lecturing his parents on how mistreated he was. "You don't love me like the others. You think I am dumb. Why am I always the one to blame?" It all settled down with the parents apologizing and the kid stomping off to brood until the parents expressed proper contrition. Amazing! Brilliant—in a wicked sort of way.

Now I am well aware of the many things parents can do to cause children insecurity and hurt. But I will save that for another day. We still have a selfish, manipulative brat ruling the house and pushing his parents around by means of a festering guilt trip.

This little boy had found his parents' weakness and capitalized on it. Mom and Dad occasionally expressed just enough anger and resentment to cause them self-doubt. Sensing their lack of confidence, the boy found ways to further deepen their guilt. He knew just what to say to cause them pain. Did he have a legitimate basis for accusing his parents of being unworthy to be his head? In some cases, as is probably true with nearly all parents, yes. The parents sensed their moral inadequacy. Granted, if they had maintained clear consciences, his manipulations would have fallen flat. It was their humble sensitiveness to their own failures that caused them to relinquish the moral authority of the family to this six-year-old tyrant. It reminds us of how the coming of the law increases sin (Rom. 7).

Now the obvious solution is to tell parents to instantly become wise and discerning. If all parents were ideal Christians, no shortcomings, no hang-ups, nothing to cause guilt, then they would always have the moral strength to withstand manipulation. Christian maturity is normal, but the fact is that in most cases it doesn't come until the children are grown. Should parents wait until they are sufficiently mature and worthy before assuming command. If so, it may then be too late for the child.

"So, if I am not the perfect parent, am I going to abdicate the throne to my imperfect child?" If your child is smart enough to touch your weak spots and make you feel guilt, is he thereby more righteous, more wise? Remember, he is using his parent's weaknesses to silence them and eliminate their interference so he can act in selfish and unruly ways. I will remind you that parenthood is not an appointed office; it is not by the consent of the child. Parents hold an office (parenthood) that carries with it certain obligations and authority apart from their worthiness. For the sake of your children, you must act now. You must rise above feelings of inferiority or unworthiness. By "rise above," I mean you must act for the child's benefit, whether you feel up to the task or not.

In our observation of this family, we detected that the mother was a very "sensitive" person. She was the first to feel the child's "emotional pain." She shied away from confrontation until suppressed frustration provoked her to act. She never spoke with authority or conviction—frustration, yes, but not with dignity and authority. She ASKED the children to comply. She "patiently" coaxed and compassionately pleaded with them. When they ignored her suggestions, she would then become exasperated and reach an impasse, where she felt overwhelmed, defeated.

As is often the case in similar situations, this mother was abused when a child. She was always fearful of not being sensitive and patient enough. She didn't trust herself. She didn't trust her husband—though she would say she did. She was fearful of failure. Her six-year-old boy was none of this. He was not broken in spirit, as he often portrayed. He just knew how to hurt his mother and short-circuit her interference with his indulgence. He was emotionally stronger than she was.

What of the father? As is the normal industrialized curse, he was away from home most of every day. Feeling out of touch, in most cases he naturally deferred to his wife's judgment. He did have more control over the children, but the pattern was set and habits formed during the two-thirds of the day when the kids were under her tutelage. He, too, stood back with insecurity when he saw the "deep hurt" of his son. He felt guilty for not being there more of the time, for dumping the load on his wife. The parents had good hearts. They were just blinded by their own fear and sense of helplessness.

One day we were sitting in the living room discussing an event that had just occurred, when their oversized dog attempted to interrupt. The father, hardly looking at the dog, commanded him to go down stairs. He didn't raise his voice, and there was no anger. He spoke with authority, expecting the dog to obey without further word or attention. The dog took off downstairs like he just heard a call to chow. I realized that in this quiet-spoken home, I had never heard either parent speak to their children with the same confident authority.

What solution did we offer this couple? We told the mother particularly, *"Get tough; you are thinking more of your own feelings than you are the needs of your children. Don't let your past hurts come into the present to continue hurting your children. You are allowing your abusing father to abuse your children through your continuing reaction."*

Right in the middle of confrontations, we guided the parents through responses to their children. *"Quit asking,"* we would say, *"Tell him what to do, and put a little toughness in you voice."* Then we would tell her, *"Don't tell him again; respect your own word; get your switch and apply it right where he stubbornly sits; ignore his self-pity. Don't assure him of your love; assure him of your authority. You are in the right; put your shoulders back and act like a commanding officer whose word is final. Do not negotiate or explain. Mother, take the whine out of your voice, and put some steel in your posture. Stay calm, but unmoving."*

The kid was amazed to discover that no one cared for his manipulating pity shows. One word from a parent was the last word—no repeat, no appeal, and no regret. It took three days, but when the child realized he had no recourse, he obeyed the first time and kept his mouth shut. By the end of the week, he was expressing more love and appreciation for his mother than he had ever shown. He began to admire her rather than see her as a weakling whom he could control. It was a joy to see and share in their victory.

Their youngest boy, age two or three, had a tough hide that at times absolutely resisted all control. He would whine, and gripe, and cry, and plead, and demand. He was a tough nut to break, but it was a simple procedure that didn't hurt anyone but the parents.

Again, it was the lack of resolute authority that cultivated whining in this two-year-old. Since the parents were seldom decisive, the child had learned that begging and pleading often caused them to capitulate to his will. When they said, "No," it was just the starting point in negotiations. After reading our book, on several occasions the parents had attempted to exert their authority and hold out against his demands, but this tough little campaigner had always endured.

Late one night we were riding back from a seminar when the little fellow noticed that he was on the other end of the seat from his mother. He was riding in a restraining seat, and so whined to sit in his mother's lap. The father SUGGESTED that it would be best if he stayed strapped into his restraining seat. The mother began to sympathetically explain why she couldn't hold him. Based on past experiences, he knew that this was just the opening round. Their rejection of his proposal was only tentative. They were just testing the waters to see if he would yield. If by continual insistence he should demonstrate how very important this issue was to him, they would eventually come around to seeing it his way. As he pleaded further, asking for water, I could see that the mother was feeling guilty for not being close to HER BABY. Didn't his tears demonstrate how important this was to his emotional well-being? After six or eight rounds, it finally reached the brokenhearted crying stage.

Mother was reaching for her baby when the father turned to me and asked, "What should I do?" Again I explained the principle—by allowing the child to dictate terms through his whining and crying, you are confirming his habit of whining and consenting to his technique of control. So I told the daddy to tell the boy that he would not be allowed to sit in his mother's lap, and that he was to stop crying. Of course, according to former protocol, he intensified his crying to express the sincerity of his desires. The mother was ready to come up with a compromise. "He was hungry. He was sleepy. He was cold." Actually, he was a brat, molded and confirmed by parental responses. I told the Father to stop the car and without recourse give him three to five licks with a switch. After doing so the child only screamed a louder protest. This is not the time to give in to demand. After two or three minutes, driving down the road listening to his background wails, I told the father to COMMAND the child to stop crying. He only cried more loudly. At my instruction, without further rebuke, the father again stopped the car and spanked the child. Still screaming, we continued for two minutes until the father again commanded the child to be quiet. Again, no response, so the car was again stopped and the child spanked. This was repeated for about twenty miles down a lonesome highway at 11:00 on a winter night.

When the situation began to look like a stalemate, the mother suggested that the little fellow didn't understand. I told the father to command the boy to stop crying immediately or he would again be spanked. The boy ignored him until Father took his foot off the gas, preparatory to stopping. Understanding the issues well enough to know that the car was stopping for the purpose of giving him a spanking for crying, he dried it up immediately. The family was relieved to have him stop and the father started to resume his drive. I said "No, you told him he was to stop crying immediately or you would spank him; he waited until you began stopping. He has not obeyed; he is just beginning to show confidence in your resolve. Spank him again and tell him that you will continue to stop and continue to spank until you get instant compliance."

The boy was smart. He may not have feared Mama. His respect for Daddy was growing, but that big hairy fellow in the front seat seemed to be more stubborn than he was, and with no guilt at all. This time when Daddy gave his command, the boy dried it up like a paper towel. The parents had won and the boy was the beneficiary.

Now you may wonder why I did not tell the father to tell the boy that he was going to spank him until he stopped crying, and so, not resume driving until he had stopped. Never put yourself in the place where you may lose the contest. What if the boy didn't stop? Would you spank him forever, or would you stop when it bordered on the abusive, in which case the child would win? Your word would fall to the ground; you gave-in before he did. You would have actually hardened his resolve to rebel. Furthermore, when a child is being spanked and shortly thereafter, he may be too emotionally wrought to make responsible decisions. Our concern is not just to silence the child, but to gain voluntary submission of his will through respect for our command.

Father tells the boy to stop crying or he will stop the vehicle and spank. Father stops, spanks, the child cries, and the father resumes the drive, waits three to five minutes, ignores the crying and continues to talk as if all is well. Five minutes later, the father again commands the child to stop crying. By this time there is no lingering pain and he has had time to quiet in his emotions and reflect on the parental mandate—"Stop crying or get a spanking." Again, the father commands the child to stop crying or he will receive a spanking. The child continues crying only because he assumes that the status quo continues. That is, he is not at all convinced that the father means what he says. Judging from past experiences, he is sure that he will win this contest eventually. By breaking it up into several sessions, the father is reprogramming the child—Father commands with a threat; child disobeys; Father carries out threat; child loses and suffers the consequences; it is an unpleasant experience; repeat all of above five to ten times. The child concludes: There is a new order; Father is consistent; he always means what he says; boy cannot win; there is no alternative to instant obedience. Get smart, be a survivor, just say no to self-will.

The beauty of this kind of contest is that when the parents conquer, it applies across the board. The child is not just yielding to the circumstances; he is yielding to his parents. The rebel in him is dying. This submission will translate into every aspect of their relationship. The child has learned that the parents have more resolve than he does. They are not liars. When they say stop or else, they mean it. There is no way to bend the parents; their word is final.

The next day we were sitting in the living room when the mother gave the little fellow a command. Out of habit, he commenced his whine, which turned to a cry. Mother looked discouraged and turned to me asking, "What should I do now?" I said, "Tell him to dry it up instantly and to start smiling." When she commanded him, he immediately stopped crying and gave a faked smile that quickly turned to a sincere one in reflection to the delight on his mother's face. I never will forget. She started laughing with absolute abandonment. She was overjoyed. "He has never obeyed me like that," she said. For the few days that remained, he obeyed her instantly and the household was a very peaceful place. The battle was won. Whether or not the victory continued depends on how consistent the parents were. The hard part was over. If the parents didn't revert to their old responses, the child wouldn't revert to his.

There are those of you who will think that the twenty miles of spanking was cruel. Remember, this was not a daily event; it was a "war to end all wars." The spankings were not wild, violent affairs. They were not greatly painful. They were done in quiet calm and dignity. It is not the severity of the spanking but the certainty of it that gives it persuasive power. Our object in spanking is not to cause the child to so fear the pain that he obeys. It is to gain the child's attention and give him respect for the parent's word. I know that there are abusive, angry parents out there who, through their own inconsistency, find themselves in a position where they excessively spank every day. Spanking should just be part of a training program. It is our consistency that trains. The rod just gives credibility to our word. If your word is not credible, no amount of the rod will ever be effective. You will become abusive. If you feel abusive, you probably are. Abusiveness resides in the mind and heart, not the switch. Get counsel and advice from a close friend who has a Biblical perspective on child training.

In reflecting on our one-week stay with this fine family, I am amazed at their humility and grace. Giving us full license in the home must have been like the Judgment Seat of Christ. Well, not quite, but about as close to it as can be had down here in the flesh. One word of warning: Don't invite us to come stay with you for a week; this old man has had all the crying and whining he can stand for the next five years. We're retired.

"Honey, I'll put some wood on the fire and you put the tea on. We'll have another quiet evening writing." ☺

Dear mike and Debi,

A friend gave me the Feb/Mar issue of No Greater Joy. What a blessing and another confirmation from the Lord. We were in the middle of pulling our child out of the Christian School. It had been a long and difficult decision as we said we would never do it. The change in our child after only 2 weeks of homeschooling has been remarkable. We are looking forward to reading what we ordered.
J.S.

The Doer of the Word

Although the man was old and stooped, he walked with the urgency of driven youth. I wonder, is it altogether a tiring body that makes an old person amble along, or is it that the man of age has reached a point of knowing that the demanding things of youth are not important after all, certainly not so important as to hurry? But this old man had either not come to such a wise state, or he had discovered something that still mattered. As he walked up that rough path strewn with rock, the morning sun was beginning to break over the mountains revealing the tiny hut the old man had just left. The freshness of the morning sun streamed through his white, downy hair, giving it a halo effect. His skin, although burned bronzed, was not that of a Mexican or Indian. Except for the few things he carried in a small native, handmade net bag he had strung over his shoulder, he had nothing with him. The path into the mountains where he walked led only to remote villages, the closest, still a day's walk. This village is what is referred to as a "nothing village"—no store, no fresh water, and only the poorest of people scratching the barren rock for substance. Why a gringo would be going that way without any provisions was a mystery to those watching him disappear up the steep trail.

"Ha! They wonder about me yet. How many years, Lord, have we been walking these trails? We first walked this very trail over 35 years ago. Those people living in the mountains are nothing people to the villages below, but I know, and You know Lord, they belong to You. How I thank you for giving to me the opportunity to be the first to tell them the sweet, sweet story. Oh, yes, I remember that day as if it were yesterday: the looks of joy on their faces as they heard the good news of salvation. Yes Lord, thank you for that wonderful harvest. Oh, it has been good to watch them grow and spread the gospel to their own people all over these mountains.

Let's see, I guess there are over two hundred churches established in these mountains now. What a harvest; how I praise you! Oh, the riches of your mercy are past finding out. Lord, I'm getting old, I don't guess I'll ever get to visit the last twenty-five churches; they are so far in the mountains. I do wish there was a place for a small airstrip. Oh well, they really don't need me, it's just that I would like to see with my own eyes what you've done.

I tell you Lord, every time I think of cutting a new airstrip I think of that time I dropped my little boy off in the middle of the mountains down south. I have to say Lord, I smile every time I remember that, but I sure wasn't smiling then. I was scared to death of having  *to tell his mother, "I lost our 10-year-old son in the mountains somewhere." "How," she would say, "could you lose a 10-year-old boy out of an airplane?" She has been a good woman, Lord, a mighty good woman. Man never had a helpmate that helped as much as mine has, and her with polio all these years. Having all those kids, schooling them, living in some of the roughest conditions, having people in her home day in and day out; she has been a good one. Bless her Lord, give her strength to finish her course. And thank you again Lord, she sure has been a sweet lady. You are a good God. But I'm telling you Lord, I was sweating having to tell her I left our boy behind to show the gospel film and when I came back to that remote Indian village a week later, the locals had taken him to the next village over. When I got to that village, he had moved on to the next. I tell you Lord, I didn't think my old rickety airplane or my fuel, not to mention my heart, was going to last through that one. Excuse me for laughing Lord, every time I remember finding him in that new village, where no missionary had ever gone, I just have this uncontrollable urge to throw my hands in the air and laugh with thanksgiving and praise. To think, my young 10-year-old son started a new work all by himself. Yes, Lord, thank you for giving me back my boy that day. He has been a blessing.*

You know Lord, I think he told me the other day he has over 80 thousand people now enrolled in correspondence in Guatemala. What a ministry! He has been like Elisha, with a double portion. Thank you Lord for a son like that. Yes Lord, thank you for all 5 of my kids. Hard to believe they are all over 30 years old now. I tell you Lord, if I can't do all the ministry I had my heart set on, it is mighty satisfying seeing my own sons and daughters doing it. Such a blessing Lord—such a blessing. Thank you Lord, for using every one of my children to your honor and grace. Yes, you have been so good.

Oh Lord, help me to remember to read the book that that man has been after me to read; that deeper life book by that China man. I guess I need to do that Lord, but I'm getting old and there is so little time left to reach this last people group over in the far southwest. Now Lord, I got an idea to air drop a bunch of tracts; say about ten thousand or so over eight of their villages. I know no one has written their language yet, but I heard some of those folks come out of the mountains to trade, and they have to know some Spanish. So the way I figure it, if the people find a strange piece of paper, they will take it to someone that might know how to read Spanish. It's an idea, Lord. You let me know if it is from You. I'm running out of time and there are still so many who have never heard. Lord, right now raise up someone to go to those tribes. You told us to pray for laborers and I want to go on record again, Lord; we need some hard working, hard walking man to finish these mountains. I'll tell them at this next meeting and maybe someone will decide to stop waiting for a lightening bolt and just obey your last command.

You know Lord I hate to have to go back to the States to another one of those meetings. They bore me to tears, spending half the night fussing about little differences. They are almost as bad as those seeking the mind of God about fasting meetings and never just opening the Book. Excuse me, Lord, I'm laughing again. Those folks don't know what fasting is, do they Lord. You remember that time I was up in—now I can't even remember where we were that time, Lord—but anyway, I'd been without food so long, I was tempted to try the stones for bread. I sure was glad that Indian family showed up with tortillas. Best tasting stuff I ever ate. Yes, Lord we have had some mighty lean times, I tell you. I've eaten all kinds of dogs, snakes, lizards, and other critters in my day—talking about unclean meat, but I guess its best to not tell those folks that kind of stuff. Might scare them off from going. Of course, not many folks are doing any going anyway. Too busy preaching about going deeper or fussing about some doctrine.

Well, Lord, I was going to ask you about this problem I've run into about the translation of these people's Bible. I need some wisdom here, Lord; you know I really want these people to know Your Word. Ouch! I wish I had my young legs back; and Lord about the village over in the south....

This story is based on fact, though the conversation with God is imagination. As of February 2001, he and his wife are still behind the plow, being "doers of the word and not hearers only." ☺

Mr. and Mrs. Pearl,

I wanted to just write a "quick" note thanking you for your obedience to the Lord in training up godly families. ...Oh, yes, I must tell you my boys too are changing dramatically from their training. It is so nice not to have to use the rod for every little thing. I can see the fear is melting away from their eyes. For instance, our 7-year-old son is always "sick" or "injured." So we whipped up some "Cure All" from vinegar, cinnamon, garlic, curry, and hot sauce. The first day he was given a dose of "Cure All" every time he complained about a scratch, not feeling good, headache.... He stopped real quick. The next day we took it further. He is quite dramatic, so he progressed from verbal statements to body language. He walked through the kitchen with his shoulders drooping, so I said, "Caleb, you look as if you don't feel good. Have some 'Cure All,' it will help." He took it and shuddered as it went down. That was the end of ANY complaints!!! It's been 4 days or so and he is smiling, happy and enjoying life. What a miracle!! And not one spanking!!!

Thank you so much.
Roxanna

A Stinking Situation

Here at The Church At Cane Creek, incidents arise from time to time amongst our young people and children that reflect upon their personalities and character. One such recent episode bears repeating, in hopes that you will be forewarned and therefore guard against a similar crisis in your community. I will admit that the children involved were too young to realize the dire consequences of their misdeed, but at what age does accountability begin?

I have hesitated to make this known publicly lest I provide further material for those who need very little to concoct juicy stories designed to cast a shadow upon our ministry. But, knowing that the story will likely leak out and cause a stink, I have decided to give you the uncensored facts before you hear a garnished version from one of our self-installed enemies. There are ample witnesses to testify to the truth of what I here write.

Recently, during a workday on a certain homestead, while the adults were preoccupied, the younger children were playing down by the stream away from the house. It was a mixture of boys and girls, all under ten years old. You know how boys and girls often compete. The boys had made a bridge across the stream and would not let the girls cross over unless they could guess the password—which they were unable to do. On the other side of the stream was a wonderful mud slide about six feet tall and very steep. I am sure it was nothing like what they have at Six Flags, but the girls thought they should share in the boy's fun. Eventually, the girls constructed their own bridge and established a password (as the eagle flies south to Australia) which the boys were unable to break. But, even though the girls now had their own access to the other side of the stream, the boys, led by Joseph, seven years old, continued to deny the girls access to the wonderful mud slide.

As the adults later gathered to consider the events that led up to the crises, it is clear that if this kind of behavior is allowed to continue, it could lead to a bloated male ego, not to mention the female's diminished sense of self-assertion.

As events developed, Joseph, the main culprit, felt the call of nature and departed for the outhouse (for you city-slickers that's an outside toilet). Emily, cute as a button and small for her four years, and otherwise normally quite passive, had endured all of Joseph's bossing she could stand. So at a discreet distance, she followed him to the outhouse. When he was securely seated inside, she slipped up and locked the door. When he got ready to leave, she was already across his bridge and sliding down his exclusive mudslide. His cries of distress, occasionally punctuated with gagging sounds, surely reached her across the field and over the creek. But I suppose her heart had been hardened by the many times of humiliation she had suffered at his uncaring hands. She continued to enjoy the slide until someone else heard the choking, pleading Joseph and released him from his steamy, fly pestering prison.

When you must avail yourself of an outhouse, you normally hold your breath the whole time. When Joseph bolted for the door and found it locked, it must have been a rather horrible experience. I am sure he will be traumatized for life. It will probably call for an entirely new field of psychiatry to treat his putraphobia.

To top it all off, the parents involved only stopped working long enough to laugh. Emily escaped with a mild reprimand that in my estimation will only encourage her in her feminist agenda.

Well now you have the whole story, as embellished as I know how. I can't imagine how this story will sound by the time it gets around. But let no more be said; this is an open and shut and open again case of good country fun. ☺

Pearls,

My children really appreciate the "unschooling" approach transforming our home. We used to stress "book work" continually, but now they are given much more free time to sew, quilt, cook, garden, art, woodwork, organize, wash clothes with a wringer washer (big hit!), make school tapes for their Down Syndrome brother, etc. We have seen amazing qualities and gifts in our children that we never knew existed. They are all so excited about learning. I praise God for the grace He has bestowed on our children. I have been a very stressed out mother for several reasons, but it (motherhood) is really starting to make sense to me. Getting rid of the high-pressure curriculum is a great burden lifted off my shoulders. We desire to do the Lord's will and pray that He would be glorified in us.   M & J

Man and Wife

T here is a young couple in our church who just had their first baby. They recently bought several acres of timberland, about a mile off the road. Determined to not borrow money, they built a twelve-foot by twelve-foot house to live in until they can save enough to build a larger one. Their "house" is without running water, except that which runs off the tin roof. It is without electricity, refrigerator, washing machine, sink, toilet, tub, furniture, etc. You say, "What does it have? Four walls, two windows (of a very used variety), one door, a cute little roof, a porch, a cozy loft for sleeping, and two young people just getting started in life, who hardly ever appear in public for the joy they have of just being together in their little castle.

The little lady carried her new baby to an auction last week and stayed all day, buying a refrigerator for $1.00, and a gas stove—a Proverbs 31 woman. The refrigerator is in anticipation of the day they get electricity. The stove will work off of a propane bottle. Can you imagine the joy on the face of a new bride meeting her husband coming home from work with the news that for $1.00 she has just furnished their would-be kitchen?

Before they got married the young man was extremely visible and active, always on the volleyball court or going somewhere with the fellows. Now, when he comes home from his construction job, he greets his wife and picks up his little baby girl. His big, rough hands completely encompass the tiny infant. The way he carries on, you would think that he is the one who gave birth. I have never seen a more intense case of male bonding with his new infant.

When she was large with child, they came over one night for us to drill them on natural home delivery. There are several midwives in the community, all work free, but they had studied and were determined to have their baby alone, just the two of them, in their little cabin. They received a lot of criticism, but they didn't notice. They continued in faith and sobriety, believing they *"would be saved in child bearing,"* just like God said.

Three days after our little child birthing class, they drove up and he jumped out with a bundle in his hands. She followed him in, and they told us of her easy delivery just a few hours earlier. They stayed with us for one day and night to shower and recover, and then returned to their homestead.

It has been several weeks now. Just the other night, the sleeping baby stopped breathing. They artificially restored respiration. It took an hour for the baby to begin breathing normally and without assistance. They didn't panic. They prayed and applied the emergency treatment he had learned in a class taken years earlier.

The joys, pains, highs and lows, the fear, the faith. Each new life, each new couple is a fresh creation, unexplored territory, mystery waiting to be discovered anew. Each life is an original creation, each couple a new Adam and Eve, each home another garden of Eden, children of God destined to be conformed into the image of God's son. God made Adam incomplete and then brought to him the woman that could cause him to grow into all that he was designed to be. She was his helper, the other half of humanity, two pieces of a whole that would bear fruit to reproduce itself and multiply the sons and daughters of God.

A book is being written. It is a great sweeping epic that carries across the centuries, covering every culture and language. Each couple is part of the cast, each event part of the script. How they play their roles will form the pages of history and define eternity. If it has been a long time since you were innocent and gullible. If bitterness and discouragement have taken the seats where hope and joy once sat, know that as long as there is life there is hope. Circumstances don't rule; attitudes do. There is no ground in which faith cannot grow. Hope doesn't need to see.

This little mother told of a lesson she learned early in marriage.

They are both athletic and decided to take a cross-country bicycle trip for their honeymoon. I must admit, such a thought never occurred to me. She related how they immediately began arguing. The husband is very stubborn, especially when it comes to reading a map. He was always (according to her) taking the wrong road—with the utmost confidence. She would say, "No, this is the right direction," and so they would argue about it. No, it is no big deal to take the wrong road when driving; you can just go twenty miles down the road and then turn around. But if you are peddling up all the hills—well....

She tells how she finally learned her role as helper. She decided that her husband couldn't read a map half as well as she could, but if he read the map incorrectly and they went in a different direction than intended, then it was God's will for her to joyously follow, lending all assistance. If he read the map incorrectly, then God would work it for their good. With that attitude, when she followed her husband, she always went in the right direction and always ended up where she ought to be—whether he did or not. They are growing. She is learning to be a good helper, and he is learning to be a more considerate leader.

It is not too late to try it again. Life still has some romance for those that will trust God and believe. ☺

Dear Mr. Pearl,

A longtime Christian friend loaned me your book. I had called her in tears knowing somewhere I had failed with my children even though they are only 4 and 2. At the time I had bruises all over my arms from the rage and rebellion of my 4-year-old son. My husband sleeps during the day and works at night. So I am the parent with our children most often. I had tried spanking, time out, bribes, bargaining, yelling, and modern "psychology." My children were utterly confused by my lack of consistency. After reading your book I realized I was destroying my children by not giving them the training that is imperative. It will probably be boot camp around here for awhile. The war I am waging is to reclaim my children for Christ. I have tried the secular discipline and now realize as with all things that the only way is God's way.

Thank you, L. A.

Return of the Volleyball Bawler

As I sat on the sidelines of the volleyball court, I observed a good example of child training. A young mother of three children was playing ball when she saw her eighteen-month-old daughter being steered toward the court by a small child about five years old. They were coming from across the grounds where the children had been playing. The little one was not crying, but all her body language indicated she had been in distress. When she got within hollering range, the five-year-old began to explain that the little one had fallen on the ground. When the eighteen-month-old became aware that her mother was now focused on her, she began to cry in earnest. At this point I started taking mental notes. Would the mother train her child to be independent and tough, or would she train her to be a crybaby and a whiner?

As the mother stopped playing and showed some concern, the child increased the volume of her crying. When the mother hollered to her that it was alright, that she should return to her playing, the cry then became desperate and defiant. The demand in the little voice was quite evident. It was not an "I'm hurt and in pain." It was a "you'd better pay attention to me, or I'll make you wish you had."

Watching this all-too-familiar proceeding, they had my full attention. Would the little girl control her mother? Would guilt move the mother to inappropriate action? The child was no longer hurting. She didn't need medical attention. She did not cry until she saw her mother looking at her. Her crying increased as a means of enforcing her desire for attention. People were now looking on. How are mothers supposed to act in a situation like this? "What do they expect me to do?" The question a mother should be asking is, "What is best for my child?"

This mother has developed some wisdom from her previous children, so, as she left the court, she pulled a switch from a tree. The little girl, seeing her mother's response, suddenly diminished her crying. By the time the mother got to the child, she had stopped crying altogether. Mother made one token swat at the child and then spoke a word of exhortation, which included, "Stop crying and go back to playing." The swat had hardly made contact and did not invoke further crying. Quite the contrary, the little girl immediately dried it up and turned to play.

Now you may be impressed with this level of control. Many of you would be glad to have as much control as this mother. But I want you to know that this is only half training. While this mother was training her daughter to stop crying, she was also training her to commence crying and wait for a rebuke—only then would she stop crying. If you could end every whining/crying spell with a quick rebuke and a token swat, you would feel successful. But what if you trained her so that when she fell down or when there was a potentially distressful situation, the child just got up, dusted herself off, and continued to play? Wouldn't that be much better?

Remember the rule of child training: Never reward the child's undesirable behavior and it will ceases to be desirable to him. Children repeat actions that give some measure of reward. The reward need not come every time. One time out of ten is enough for a child to keep trying. That mother is either not consistent, or her responses are not sufficiently negative. The child would stop her demanding wail and her stumbling, pitiful presentation to mother if it were always without reward.

Back to our illustration. When the mother stopped playing and approached the child with kindly rebuke and a token swatting, the child did, in a small measure, get her way. She may have hoped for more, and may occasionally get more, but that little attention is sufficient to keep her whining and keep her returning for the ten seconds of attention.

You may feel sympathy for the child and say, "Well the poor child obviously needs attention; the mother should give it to her." Yes, children need much attention, but should they be allowed to demand it with a whine or a pretended hurt? If you allow such to be the occasion for affection, you are perverting something wholesome. You are reinforcing negative behavior. Those of us who have been parents for a while and have successfully raised kids are not impressed with children's self-pity. They will get the attention they need, but not on such warped terms.

How could the mother entirely eliminate this negative behavior? Do not give the child any of what she wants. Tell her to stop crying,

"Now!," and without making sympathetic eye contact, go to her and switch her on the leg (one lick) so that it hurts, and as you turn away, over your shoulder say, "Stop crying and go play." Don't give her any of what she wants, and make sure that what you do give her will be unpleasant. When she is convinced that you will no longer reward her demands, she will cease demanding. There is a time to give attention and a time to withhold attention. Give the child attention when you want to reinforce behavior, and withhold attention when the behavior is negative. If you must respond in a corrective manner to negative behavior, make sure that there is no reward in it for either of you. Get tough Mama. Ask, "What is best for my child?" And then ask God to give you the courage to do it. ☺

Dear Michael and Debi

We have enjoyed your books. Thank you for your insight. I wish you could visit a few days for a critique. We are making changes in our lifestyle and attitudes towards parenting and marriage roles (Me, obey Him????!).

I began listening to the "For Men Only" tape that I ordered for my husband-sorry. My seven-old-son was in the room and heard the warning that a wife could ruin her marriage by listening to the tape. I promptly turned off the tape (rewound it and wiped off my grungy fingerprints). My son was very concerned and said, "Boy, I sure am glad you turned that off. You could have ruined your marriage!"

Winnie

Barbie Dolls or Baby Dolls?

$\mathbf{M}$any parents have expressed concern over Barbie-like dolls. Other mothers defend Barbie by pointing out that they enjoyed the dolls without any harm. "It didn't hurt me," is the usual reply. I wonder, Mama, if indeed it didn't hurt you. Do you sometimes have a strange, sexually compelling thought life? I have talked to many women who confess the struggle they have with lustful daydreams, imagining themselves to be sexy, beautiful dolls (a most appropriate word in this case). Yet they confess to not functioning well with their own husbands. What is the root of their problem? What caused make-believe to be more satisfying than the real world? Could it be they were trained from a small child to play make-believe (daydream) when they were given a sexy little doll to dress and undress?

Many would argue that Barbie-type dolls are not sexy, but the real world says something else. It is very common in men's prisons and military barracks to find Barbie dolls in various stages of undress sitting in prominent places. It is a kind of hands-on pornography which they seem to find very gratifying. Did you know that some of the biggest fans of Barbie Dolls are middle-age men?

Somehow, parents are badly deceived, and their children are the victims. Think about it, Mother. Would you invite a 20-year-old, over-endowed model to come into your daughter's room to be admired for her body and dress? Would you allow your daughter to help her dress? Strange to even write something like that, yet that's what Barbie represents.

It is a healthy and natural instinct for little girls to love babies and to imagine themselves in the role of a loving mother. Role-playing is real preparation for the future, but there is absolutely no similarity between playing **baby** dolls and playing Barbie dolls. They are two different kinds of dolls with two different purposes. What are you training your little girl to be? When and how will she finally realize the dreams stimulated by Barbie? Would Jesus give a Barbie doll to a little girl? You have been warned. ☺

Movers or Shakers?

M any need a community, a church, a sanctuary, a new start, a place to save their marriage or their children.

American Christians are in the midst of a cultural shift. We see it everywhere: the letters we receive, those we meet when we are doing seminars, periodicals, magazines, and books. It is a movement that has by no means peaked. Before it is over, most Christians will have gone the way of corruption. But a minority, which will still number in the hundreds of thousands, will get out of the destructive vortex. It reminds me of the westward movement in wagon trains. Everything is left behind and all is risked for the sake of a fresh start, a new world.

Without any help from us, several families have looked us up and moved into our community. Out of the sixteen families that now make up the Church, only five are indigenous. Twelve families, including our own, are transplants. We are from Memphis, Louisiana, Florida, Colorado, North Carolina, Alabama, Wisconsin, Ohio, North Dakota, some singles from Mississippi, New Mexico, Texas, and my memory fails me. We are all escapees, fleeing the world and its influences. We each brought our own unique problems and blessings.

Migrating to create Christian communities is an inevitable trend as Christians continue to scream, "Stop the world, I want to get off." But I warn you, the romance eventually goes out of everything except a good marriage. We recently lost two families. They found that their needs were not being met. We failed to live up to their expectations. I think some others are disappointed. The magic never happened. Eventually, they will move on, again looking for someplace where they are not. Have you heard about the man who, out of a desire to escape his past, added a new room to his house so he could have a sanctuary not contaminated with the past? To keep it from being corrupted, he allowed no outside influence, no magazines or electronic media, and no visitors. On the day of its completion he hurriedly closed himself in, whereupon he found himself in a museum of his own life. He soon discovered it to be generally of a lower quality than the world he had shut out. How far do you have to travel to become someone else? What State is the state of contentment? Where is that community with people not made of flesh? Where can you find a group of young people who never grow up to question everything? New homes don't make new families.

Many communities such as ours have sprung up all over the country—back-to-basics folks. Some have goats, chickens, cows; a few try plowing with horses. Not far from us is a community of 150, all living on one farm in two houses. They are seeking to recover something they feel is lost. I am sure it will get stepped on before they find it. My wife recently talked with a leader of a church/ community movement, and he told her that they are turning people away. He said, "I send them places where I don't agree with all the doctrine; we just cannot contain them." This past week a man told me how he tried to join another community in Ohio, but they sent him away. "We have enough already," he was told. Weekly, families drift through who are looking for the "recovered church." I tell them, "You won't find it here; we are the Church of Laodicea— lukewarm." The entire spectrum runs from those hoping to survive the Great Tribulation to those hoping to survive the greater tribulation of marital relationships. If they are saved, they will never see the Great Tribulation. If they are married they must learn to endure unto the end of the tribulation of their own making. For those who are hoping that a community of believers will deliver them, the rapture is their only hope on both accounts.

By phone, by letter, when we go out speaking, many times I hear, "We are looking for families of like mind; where we live we are not understood." In most cases they have a valid concern. They are correct in their rejection of the culture they live in. But, is the answer found in building a retreat with others of like mind? Obviously we feel it is a valid option, for we as a family have somewhat taken that course.

I have gone to large churches in major cities and met small fellowships, communities even, of believers who have taken steps to isolate themselves and sanctify their environment. They have picked their friends carefully. They homeschool, teach their children the biblical approach to marriage, and have family worship. They are a church inside of a church. They usually view the larger church, with its age segregation and youth activities, as a threat to their sanctification. Many are turning to house churches. The cream is leaving structured Christianity and starting over again.

But I am seeing a general failure of this new phenomenon of the Christian community to achieve the hoped for goals. How many families must one search through to find ten who would be ideal examples to your children? I don't mean selecting them from a magazine cover or from a stage at a family-life convention. If, from a hundred thousand families, ten such were carefully selected, would they also select yours? Would you be content to live in a community of families just like your own, where all the women respond to their husbands just as you do, where all men have the same patience and discipline as you, where all the children are just as creative and spiritually minded as your own?

The families who have moved here all have unrealized needs they hope the church will supply. When a family leaves their church looking for a better one, I often wonder how much the church they left behind is going to miss their ministry. When you get any fifteen families together with the accompanying sixty-five kids, you have a whole spectrum of problems. What is the church? Is it an exclusive club of selected families for support purposes, or is it all of those whom Christ has added to His body? Who decides who is in the church, men or God? If the ideal club existed, who would want to join it—those who had no needs and much to offer, or those who are desperate and hoping to stop their dangerous slide? Would you turn away the desperate, or would you flee from them and regroup in a purged and selected group? How long will it last? Will you appoint a committee to screen new applicants? How long will it be before you feel the need to flee from them, or they from you? I am not suggesting that you stay where your family is suffering at the hands of the world, but have you considered doing something about it, starting in your own home?

The Church is in retreat. It is backing up, withdrawing its troops and hoping to salvage that which remains, but its small reserves are dwindling. The love of many is waxing cold. Blame and accusations are thrown around everywhere. Everything is too big, too fast, too impersonal. Where did America go? The big impersonal cities have eaten the communities. Any magazine with a peaceful, idyllic scene is an instant hit. People pay a high price for dreams. For many, the only sanity left is in their imaginations. The "tie that binds" is no longer family; it is unwelcomed economic responsibilities and worldly associations.

There needs to be a change, but there are so many weak and

wounded Christians with the bless-me mentality. They are looking for a church, or a man, or a community to minister to their needs. Looking to the church for your family's spiritual health is like watching organized sports to get your exercise. No church or community can reclaim your family, restore your marriage, or assure your children of godliness. The father is the spiritual head, not the single source, but the leading member in religious instruction and example. Life begins in the home, not the church. You can't move into holiness, or join holiness, or associate yourself with holiness. If holiness is not in your soul in the worst of circumstances, it will surely fade when times are ideal. The hardest place to be an overcomer is where there is little to overcome except that which is within.

In conclusion, if your family is going downhill, and you've not been able to turn it around, I can understand your desperation. Many families have found it a great help to move away from the fast pace, to get out of debt, to turn back to a simpler way of life, to devote more time to family, worship, and ministry. Others have tried to make such a move and found that they took all their problems into their new lifestyle. God changes men's hearts, not their houses. He starts on the inside, where we start on the outside. While we are blaming the influence of others, God is waiting on us to bear the right influence to others. The power of the gospel is not limited. If you are not experiencing the gift of new life where you are, moving won't help.

It is the take-charge attitude that will make a difference. Don't run from your neighbors. You may need to disentwine your families, but then take steps to change them with the power of the gospel. Don't spend all your time teaching your children how to dodge the world. Teach them how to change it with the love of God and a King James Bible. In these last days before the close of this age, we don't need to retreat in order to survive, but rather advance in order to save. We are in the flesh, but we do not war after the flesh. We are in the world, but not of it. God took us out of the world so He could send us back into it with a message and an example. If, in fear of the world, you spend your time criticizing it, you are as much a victim as those who love it. Stop being merely a complainer and become more than a conqueror through him that loved us. As long as you are in this body of flesh, you will never be able to move away from the world, so turn around and shake it with the gospel. Whether you are a mover or not, at least be a shaker. ☺

...and Raymond begat Jubal, and Jubal was a mighty trapper in his day.

By Debi Pearl

About one year ago I stopped over at Jubal's house to pick up something. Being in my usual hurry, I hardly noticed his conversation to me, until about half way to the car when I caught the words "trapping," "skinning out," and "real soft hides." It got my attention, because at the time he was only 7 or 8 years old. "Oh, have you and your daddy been trapping?" "Naw, just me, and sometimes I let Beulah," he said, looking over at his tiny feminine sister. Sometimes I can't control my eyebrows. I could feel the pull of skin as they rose up in wonder. As he was speaking he seemed very distracted with a tiny piece of something he was diligently rubbing between his thumb and index finger. With his constant chatter, made harder to understand with the missing teeth, his wiggling around, and the activity with his hands, I was having a hard time getting all the story straight.

Trying not to appear unbelieving, I asked an intelligent question, "Are you doing the skinning, or are you helping your dad?" He looked at me with blank shock, "Do you think my dad would help me skin them?" That didn't make sense either, so I asked, "How many skins have you tanned, and are you going to sell them?" He stopped his incessant rubbing and looked skyward as he mentally counted his stock of furs, "I guess 6, counting this last one I'm working on, but you can't sell them cause there's not a market for them, but I might put them together and make something nice or just give them away." Now he had me. Busy or not I was going to see what this young man was working on. I asked, "Well, why don't you take me to see your hides, Jube? They sound very interesting." When I saw the look of appreciation on his small face, I knew I had said the right thing. Then he held out his hand, offering me the tiny object he had been rubbing. "Sure is soft and pliable fur, and it's tougher than rabbit," he explained as I examined the small piece of fur, complete with the four tiny extensions representing the legs. Horror is not the right word, but somehow words desert me as I try to remember how I felt when realization hit me. As if stuck in slow motion, I could feel a mounting tremor starting at my feet as I tried to shove the fresh hide back into his hands. "What?" was all I could utter. He had me fair and square. I think he knew the impact he had made, but he suppressed his grin as he said, "Mouse, ain't it fine?" I learned my lesson; don't stop to talk to strangers or little boys. ☺

Dear Michael and Debi

About six weeks ago, my husband and I had pretty much reached the end of our resources to train and discipline our two children. We figured they were pretty well behaved and respectful in public, but the respect level at home was deteriorating.

We were using our usual methods—spanking for outright defiance, timeouts for being disrespectful, privileges denied, etc.; they just weren't effective enough. As a new homeschooling family (kids 4 & 5), it was crucial that we have order and peace, but we didn't know how. One Wednesday night the tension came to a head, and basically my husband and I turned on each other. It was awful.

That night I prayed, "Lord, I have no idea what to do—PLEASE help us—we're drowning!" The very next day a friend came by for lunch. During the course of our visit, she said, "I brought by a couple of books—I though they were pretty good." We frequently exchange books anyway so I just took them without thinking about it. (She had NO idea of what had happened the previous night or how much we were struggling.) Later that day, I began to read To Train Up a Child and I read excerpts out loud to my husband. We both quickly realized that God had provided the solution to our problem. He blessed so much—my husband doesn't usually read books, but he took that one and read it before I did. We were both amazed and rejoiced at the answer to our prayer! In just a day we saw a difference in our children. It is much better at home now—though we are still learning. Through reading your material, God opened our eyes to the awesome responsibility of parenting. We don't want to be reactive parents anymore. Anyway, we'd like a set of your books so that we can return our friend's copy.

Gratefully, S. & K. M.

Training & Example

T here are two aspects to child training. One is technique and the other is example. Technique involves knowing what needs to be done, what method will work, and how to implement it. By example, we are referring to that worthy condition of the parent wherein the child is motivated to emulate the trainer. Example involves teaching and instruction, whereas technique can be implemented before the child is old enough to understand reason or interpret example.

Many of our readers have been instantly released from fear and frustration as they discovered the simple concepts of training. These truths are not new or profound. We are not revealing something we personally discovered. It is just that in our age, psychology and the media have erased the common sensibilities of parents; or, in many cases, parents have been caused to fear rather than to trust their own gut feelings. When you see your own deep, though previously buried, feelings in print, and you hear that there is practical truth in what you felt all along, it instantly frees you from fear and indecision. So many parents have said to us, "It's just like I knew it all along, I just couldn't put it into words."

For a child under two, technique is nearly the whole of training. This involves anticipating the kind of behavior you expect from your child and instituting deliberate events to train to that end. For example, if the first time an infant spits out his food you put it back into his mouth and say "No," repeating that action as many times as necessary until he swallows it, and you are thereafter consistent to never allow a single exception to your rule, you will not end up with a two-year-old brat that spits food. Nor will you end up with a six-year-old that is finicky and demanding about what he eats.

Technique comes from common sense and experience and does not depend on the character of the trainer. No one can plead inability to be a good trainer based on personal shortcomings. At an early age, parental example matters only to the extent that it affects the application of training techniques. If you are slothful and angry, it may rob you of the calmness required to train, but the character fault itself will not prevent you from training your child not to be angry.

Being an obese, selfish, intemperate eater yourself will not prevent you from training your small child to self-discipline. But when he is twelve, and you are demanding that he develop a little self-discipline in his eating habits, your example will be all that does matter. In other words, when children are very young, *who you are* is not as important as *what you do* by way of training. The two-year-old cannot compare values and be offended by your inconsistencies.

Now I am not saying that training can occur despite your own personal discipline in order to exempt you from the need to be a good example, but to make a point about the nature of training. Parents who rely on their own example are wasting their time with the one- to three-year-olds. Children need about three or four years of applied training technique before teaching can begin to be effective.

As children get older, they begin to develop knowledge of good and evil, and as such, example begins to play a larger part. By the time they are maybe seven or eight, example will become more important than technique. When they come to a mature knowledge of good and evil—around twelve to fourteen—technique matters little, and example is paramount.

Most parents are unaware of this growing shift in their children. Before they know it, the kids reach a point where they are no longer impressed by stern words and threats. Parents are shocked when they suddenly become aware that their children are judging them. These not-so-little children suddenly show "righteous" defiance and sling accusations back at their "hypocritical" parents. Though they may not speak it, their responses say, "Who are you to tell me what's right and wrong?" The children cease to show repentance, because they lose respect for the moral measuring stick of their parents. When they realize that their parents are demanding more than they (the parents) are willing to give, it is like finding out that there is no Santa Claus. "It was all a lie. Maybe everything is a lie." Wake up parents.

Parents are the last to see this change coming. They get comfortable in a routine that has worked well thus far. They successfully intimidated and bullied the kids into compliance. It sometimes took a while, but the bluster of the parents eventually dominated. But not anymore. It is too late for training to be effective apart from godly example. And the kids are far too mature in their knowledge of good and evil to be fooled by pretense and hypocrisy. In fact, at this fresh stage of moral awakening, children's consciences are much more sensitive and demanding than that of adults who have learned to accept a certain amount of hypocrisy and pretense as normal. Nothing gets by the kids. They will hold your feet to the moral fire.

The problem is that most parents get it backward. During the first years of a child's life when example is useless, the parents just expect the children to grow into the mold of family life. Then when

the children get old enough so their selfishness is no longer cute, parents begin to try to train them out of their bad habits.

In a family where there has been no training, the parents are angry, short fused; they often raise their voices; they are always frustrated and feel as if the kids are their adversaries rather than partners. Parents' reactions to their failure to achieve results is something rather childish itself. The kid missed training and now he has no example. When you scream at a kid to stop screaming, what is the basis of your command? Threat? When your eyes flash, your pulse soars, and impatience pours from you like a sand storm, does the command that follows carry in moral authority, or just an I'm-bigger-than-you threat? The kids started out with no training, until they were incorrigibly indulgent, and now no example, just conflict with an adult size version of themselves. You are wasting your time saying, "Do you hear me!" They don't. They can't. Your attitude is louder than your words. To wait until it becomes a problem and then try to apply enough pressure to fix it is like waiting for a flood as a signal to build a levy.

How did this parent/child crisis develop? The one- to three-year-old children are treated like houseplants. They are cleaned, watered, fed, loved, and made a source of entertainment and delight, while the parents trust to example for the child to learn established limitations and boundaries. "Children left to themselves bring their mother to shame." By the time they are three, they have not only learned all the bad habits, they have adopted them as a way of life. Unwise parents trusted to emulation, and when that didn't work they turned to intimidation. The untrained three-year-old senses the disapproval of those around him, but he doesn't have the wisdom or self-control to labor for approval. He responds to rejection and criticism with rebellion. The parents, having failed to train them when they were three months old, find them despicable terrors when they are three years old. The children are still not old enough to reason upon example and respond in kind. Their flesh is in full control with no restraints through training. When children grow to about four years old, they have assumed an adversarial role—same as the parents. The parents bear down even more with threats and punishments. At the age of six or eight the children begin to make judgments about their parents' shortcomings. At this point your life overpowers your words. By grounding, lecturing, balling out, and spanking parents think they are teaching the child right from wrong. They think they are training.

Much of the confusion and failure to this point is a result of ignorance on the part of parents. They took too much for granted and were always just a little behind the child. The child is the leader. The parents become reactors, always on the verge of meltdown. They are running along behind, disapproving and trying to pick up the pieces. They were not out front training. It is the difference between training a dog not to leave the yard or waiting until he gets a habit of doing so and then beating him for it.

So, what is the answer if you have older children and now realize you have messed up? You failed to train when they were young, and you have failed as an example. What can you do to start over? Two things. First, you must change in your own heart. Just realize that your children are not your enemies. It is your fault that they are what they are. You planted the garden and failed to weed it, then you went in with a weed eater and destroyed half the plants. Don't blame the garden. Repent. Admit your own failure and become humble. Depending on the age of your child, you will need to employ a combination of training and example. To the degree that your child can perceive your own inconsistencies, you must become a new person. Your child's bitterness will continue where you are demanding more than you are willing to be yourself. If your child is older, he/she must be brought to repentance through the goodness and example of your own heart.

Especially for children twelve or older (give or take two years) you are dealing with the soul of an adult, not adult in mind or social grace, but the soul of an adult nonetheless. You cannot override the spirit of that child. You may still have a few more years where intimidation will gain outward compliance, but the soul of the child will grow away from yours unless you get real.

Your twelve-year-old is the best psychologist in the world. You can fool your prayer partner, your counselor, your church, but you will not fool your child. You must exemplify all that you want your child to become. Your child must love your soul and desire to be a part of it. Your love and righteousness must pull admiration from your child. It is too late for impersonal training techniques. There are still some training tools available to be applied to older children, but they only enforce the communication of our souls, they do not replace it.

Parent, God is calling us to continual repentance. Our children are our ultimate fruit. A teenager is a revelation of parents. Their maturity is harvest time. The wheat and tares are made manifest. Other than a recording made in secret, children are the only failures that talk back to us, that become an advertisement of our past. Our children will be evidence, admissible in the court of heaven. Let us repent daily and walk in truth with a pure heart. Love must flow from us to all the world, encompassing our children as the early dew settles over a garden. Without love all my discipline and lectures are as the clang of a garbage truck, a truck that leaves garbage rather than picks it up.

Repent, not for the sake of your children, but for the love of your Savior who desires your pure fellowship. Repent for eternity's sake. Time is short. Repent because holiness is the pleasure of God and we are made and redeemed for holiness. Holiness is our eternal state, so enter into it as deeply as you can. God is first found at the cross, but after that, He is found enthroned in holiness. Know God if your children are to know him. Love God if your children are to love him. Repent if your children are to repent. And walk as you would have your children walk. ☺

The Reformed School of Alexandria?

W e did not raise our children in a classroom environment. I conducted my "classes" in the front seat of the pickup or in the cabinet shop. Deb conducted her classes in the kitchen or sitting at the kitchen table enthusiastically discussing points of interest to the children. They chose projects that were interesting to them. They could be found searching the library, collecting rocks, leaves, and bugs or constructing solar systems with foam balls, wire, and paint. The only tests they took were when someone tried to cheat them at a cash register or when they were dividing up earnings from a corporate entrepreneurial endeavor. Have you ever seen three kids, ages four, six, and eight dividing up $5.37? Old-fashioned suspicion will make a mathematician out of them in a hurry. I am often asked, "But aren't schools the best way to learn?" Where did you get a ridiculous idea like that?

H.G. Wells, a noted humanist and historian, wrote concerning the schools of Alexandria, Egypt, between the second and seventh centuries AD.

"Wisdom passed away from Alexandria and left pedantry [pretentious display of knowledge] behind. For the use of books was substituted for the worship of books. Very speedily the learned became a specialized queer class with unpleasant characteristics of its own. The Museum had existed for half a dozen generations before Alexandria was familiar with a new type of human being: shy, eccentric, unpracticed, incapable of essentials, strangely fierce upon trivialities of literary detail, as bitterly jealous of the colleague within as of the unlearned without—the Scholarly Man. He was as intolerant as a priest, though he had no cave. For him no method of copying was sufficiently tedious and no rare book sufficiently inaccessible. He was a sort of by-product of the intellectual process of mankind. For many precious generations the new-lit fires of the human intelligence were to be seriously banked down by this by-product."

I have observed the byproduct of America's modern counterpart to the Alexandrian school. Their frail bodies, white with the tan of florescent lights, shoulders humped, eyes squinted, poor complexion from the junk food consumed between lessons, stumble from their classrooms to stand in line for the next culturally preordained phase of life. Their mentality is that since they have given themselves to the system, the system owes them a good job, good wages, medical coverage, fair play, protection, entertainment, a vacation, retirement, old age convalescence, and a proper burial. God save us from being average. I don't want to be a part. I don't want to rear children to be a cog in this wheel.

It is obvious that many homeschooling families are nothing more than reformed public educational systems. A system faulty at the very core of its philosophy doesn't need reformation. It needs dismissal. The educational system in America doesn't need a new teacher; it needs a new birth.

Whether in the home, dictated by parents, or in the corporate classroom, John Dewey style education has taken an invasive, destructive course. Intensive, time-consuming mental discipline—out of proportion to working with the hands—is alien to natural humanity and a threat to normal development. It is a perversion to take a five- to twelve-year-old child and enter him in a demanding competition for academic excellence. We would all find fault with an ambitious adult that put his seven-year-old child through a demanding schedule of football training. Is the seven-year-old any better equipped to handle the emotional demands of professional study? How can we justify raping a child's youth by forced confinement in full time study? Child prodigies are usually abnormal, unfulfilled adults. Head-starters are often late finishers with no desire to continue their education.

Just as the motions of crawling are essential to the development of an infant, and the four-year-old hanging on to his mama's skirts is essential to a child's sense of security, so the ten-year-old following his daddy around is an integral part of his psychological development into manhood. Schooling will fill their brains with facts, enabling them to pass tests, but it will not teach them to relate to society. When children should be developing confidence, creativity, individuality, strong bodies, and work ethics, instead they are made to cease independent decision making and march (or rather sit) in formation to the drum beat of a lifeless curriculum. If you have wondered where the real men went, they disappeared into textbooks and went through puberty with books in their laps rather than tools in their hands.

Let us not go through another upper class Alexandrian Dark Age. There is no ignorance as great as book ignorance—not ignorance OF books, ignorance IN books. Just so you understand my perspective: I am a college graduate. I write this while sitting in a room with thousands of books lining all available wall space from the floor to ceiling. I have read a meaningful portion of most of them. My children all read for enjoyment and do research to satisfy curiosity or to fill a need. Rebekah, our only child who thus far has found it needful to go to college, earned a four-point average. My present purpose is not to brag on my kids. I am willing enough to do that, but I want you to understand that book education is shallow without a larger education in real life. When book education becomes predominate, the student is no longer living in the real world.

I know that there comes a time when a mature adult may need to immerse himself in studies, shutting out the real world, but this should be the burden of a mature adult who has a goal that can only be realized through the weariness of much study. A child who is yet growing and developing a personality and character should not spend long periods of time withdrawn in study.

What horrors, to see a small child quivering under the condemnation of his mother because he can't keep his mind on a dead book lying in front of him! Long hours of boredom and pretended study stunts the intellectual growth of young children. Yes, we want our children to be educationally equipped to enter into any field or discipline they may choose, but mind-set is more important than mind content. It is far more important for a child to grow into personal confidence, creativity and vision than to rush into academic excellence. The reality is that most homeschooling parents are following the current pop philosophy, sacrificing the humanity of their children for the promise of academic security.

There must be a balance. Rather than the imbalance of six hours of study and one hour of recess, for the six- to ten-year-old, let there be one hour of study, five hours of recess, and two hours of work. Balance the ten- to fourteen-year-old with two hours of play, one hour of study, and five hours of work. Balance the fifteen- to sixteen-year-old with seven hours of work, one hour of study, and let him find time to play. Following a natural course as I have described, the seventeen- to eighteen-year-old won't need your balancing; he will be a man in every sense of the word. The seventeen-year-old girl will be a lady of poise and confidence, ready to meet whatever challenges await her.

Over the last 40 years I have observed many families who believed the greater the education the greater the success in life. Many of those college graduates have never provided adequate support for their own families. Opportunity existed, but they were not able to do anything other than sit at a desk on a weekly salary. If the economy were to collapse, they would not know how to survive.

I know that what I have said is radical. A little light in a great darkness is always radical. I have not advocated ignorance. Quite the contrary. It is isolated book learning that is ignorance, ignorance of real life. College professors don't make better spouses and parents than do farmers. Corporate executives can be terribly ignorant in human relationships. Engineers can be insecure wimps who are paralyzed with fear at the thought of being cast upon their own bare resources. Politicians can negotiate a peace treaty with a foreign power but do not have the power to negotiate peace with their own teenagers. Computer programmers can solve the most complex problems but not be able to deal with the complexities of marital relationships.

The profession with the lowest divorce rate and the lowest suicide rate is that of farmer. Again, I am not advocating avoidance of the higher trained professions. I am just aware that children and young people should not be pushed by anxious parents who feel that their children's happiness depends on cramming them full of book knowledge as early as possible. When they are old enough to send themselves through college, they can make that decision to become a professional student. The self-confidence and working skills learned in their youth will better equip them for higher education than will the long hours of wimpish study in youth.

In your heart you know that the present public system is anti-human as well as anti-God. Homeschoolers have eliminated the anti-God aspect, but most of them have retained the anti-human elements in their schooling.

Children need a mother who has the time and energy to mother them, not a teacher who has neither the time nor the patience to appreciate them as people. Lay down your stern professor's mantle and pick up your apron. Next time you meet eyes with your child make sure it is with approval and not with academic disappointment. I never did like the teachers that gave out achievement tests, nor the ones who handed out the scores. In your desire to see your children "educated," don't stop being a mama or a daddy. Relax and give them time to develop emotionally. Allow them to be three years behind the normally accepted standard in academic achievement, and by the time they are sixteen they will be three years ahead. Twelve to fifteen is a very good age for "catching up." The twelve-year-old who has not developed a disposition against schooling will learn more in six months than most kids know when they graduate. A child who is confident and secure will learn with ease. Fear of failure and rejection will close the mind up worse than retardation. Many children fear learning because they associate it with painful boredom and/or rejection.

Children are all different. The beauty of homeschooling is that we can adapt to the needs of the child. Our oldest daughter, Rebekah, loved books, writing, music, art, etc. She was reading by the time she was four, but she couldn't add the change in her pocket until she was baking bread. Our next son, Gabriel, could count money before he could speak plainly. At eight-years-old he amused himself and impressed others with his simple calculations. It was nothing unusual for him, but with an older sister like he had, he thought he was pretty smart. We assured him that he was. At eight years old he could use a tape measure and help me in the shop, but he couldn't read or write at all. He just had no interest. We didn't push, but after the way Rebekah learned we were beginning to wonder if he would ever learn to read. She was writing poetry at eight years old. At eight he couldn't write his name in the mud he left on the floor.

The day finally came when he walked up to Deb and said, "I want to learn to read the Bible like Daddy." She sat down with him and opened a King James Bible—since it's the easiest one to read. Earlier he had refused phonics, seeing it had no immediate practical purpose, so she started him reading by rote from Genesis 1:1. In two weeks, one hour a day, he had learned the basics of reading. Within six months, he could read on his own, with comprehension.

Less than a year from the time he started learning to read, the State of Tennessee forced us to have the children tested. Our children had never taken a test and never been in a classroom. I had to explain to Gabriel how to conduct himself as part of an indoor society. He had to leave his throwing knives at home along with his shotgun. I explained to him that he was supposed to sit at the desk and not wander around the room examining things and asking what they were. And above all, don't speak unless spoken to. It didn't make any sense to him, but he was as game as that time he jumped off the diving board with his feet tied together and his hands tied behind his back. This was a new challenge and he loved challenges.

They arrived at the school to find stern faces greeting them. The teachers were not at all sympathetic with us and made it as hard as possible. I must say, I was nervous. I stayed home like an expectant father who didn't have the guts to go to the hospital. I had no idea how they would do. I was just hoping they could come up to their grade level. Nine-year-old Gabriel scored several years ahead of his supposed level, and eleven-year-old Rebekah scored in the upper High school to college level.

You would expect them to come home weary and emotionally drained. Mama was. But they hurriedly changed clothes and jumped in the pond. All was forgotten. While other children were still laboring through their last hours of confinement, our children were lost in the wonders of tadpoles, frogs, and flips off the diving board into the muddy water.

You can have the computer geeks and the pale faced, thin shouldered, soft bellied, bookworms. Give me a little man who can swing an ax, fix a bicycle or car, build a house, read with comprehension, and compute all the money he is making from the labor of his own strong hands. ☺

A Mother Asks...

D ear Michael and Debi,

Our son is seven years old. As soon as church lets out, the boys, young and old, are running around on the deck, out in the street, jumping on each other, and many times the "play" gets out of hand. In recent weeks things have escalated into what can almost be described as full-fledged gang war between the older and the younger boys. The older boys taunt the younger ones; the younger ones start chasing and jumping on the older ones, and someone gets hurt. We seem to be the only ones at our church that show any concern over this situation.

Many times we find ourselves intervening. Two weeks ago after an evening meeting I came around the side of the church building to find a group of five, 10- to 13-year-old boys around our son with one of them holding my son's neck from behind and smashing his face into the wall. The "mama bear" definitely came out in me and I jumped in. The older boys stated that our son had been jumping on them, etc. (which our son did confess to) but in retaliation our son had been ruffed up pretty badly.

I read with much interest "Sorry, I'm Tied Up At the Moment" (See page 30). Both my husband and I were raised with certain expectations of decorum around "grown ups." Although in an informal setting such as camping I understand that it can be great fun where these lines become relaxed. We were a bit undone one night when we had our pastor and his wife over for a visit, and our son ran in the room, jumped in the pastor's lap and started tickling him. We realized this is an area that we need to do some training, but with the situation at our church where younger boys are duking it out in the street after church with man-size older boys, it's hard for our son to distinguish where to draw the line.

I'm sorry to have been so long-winded about this, but our situation seems so different from what you described in either "A Whole Boy" or "Rowdy Boys" (See page 25 or 28 respectively). Our son is a boy that can sit still for hours. One of his favorite things to do is sit and have me read to him. He often begs for me to read "just one more chapter" long after my voice begins to wear out. We live on two and a half acres where he has all sorts of room to run, we have pigs and sheep and a pony, but like I mentioned before I often have to encourage him to go outside or stay outside with us. But here recently, when our son gets around other boys he goes a bit nuts; me too. This has all come on us so suddenly that it has really caught us off guard. We would greatly appreciate any suggestions you have to offer.

Answer

Dear Mama Bear,

It is difficult to prescribe a singular solution. Based on assumptions I make from reading your letter, I will make some suggestions that may help you make some adjustments.

The way I understand it, there are several layers to this issue, making it complex. The situation you described after church is definitely an incubator for trouble. The church leadership should take steps to eliminate the marauding herds of developing male humans. But understand, you have no control over the church. If others are not bothered, there is nothing you can do to change the overall situation. Be careful not to become a meddling nag. As to your own part, leave immediately after the service and do not allow your son to roam. If you must stay, appoint a place for him to sit until you are ready to leave.

In this area your concerns are natural and justifiable, but, if I am reading you correctly, you have complicated the problems of male youth with a common feminine over-sensitivity.

If "mama bears" had their way, baby bears would always be little biting bullies with no understanding of social give and take. Puppies, bears, and kids learn not to bite by getting bit in return.

Mamas who run interference for their little boys do two things: 1) they make weak sons, 2) they cause the other kids to continue picking on the 'bratty' little boy with the 'meddling' mama.

You mentioned his wild response when other boys come around. You are shocked at the recent change. Perhaps the change is shocking because a change that should have occurred gradually was suppressed until it burst forth suddenly. It sounds to me as if he is a late bloomer. My sons were delightfully wild by the time they were four. The only way you could get them to sit in your lap after they were five was to make them take off their knives (real knives), lay their BB guns down, and then forcibly wrestle them into your lap. Keeping them indoors was like trying to keep a dog up a tree.

If his boyhood has been subdued and is then suddenly released, it may be that neither of you knows how to handle it. Out of camaraderie, young boys will pick on older boys. The youngsters are honored when the older boys notice them. And then, it is such a challenge to test one's mettle against a stronger  opponent. It really makes a little kid feel big to bop a big guy and get away with it. If you will observe them, it is all done with laughter and great fun. But eventually the little attackers become a nuisance or maybe go too far with their 'attacks' and the big guys decide to teach them their place. The little guy may end up crying and tattling. If you are the parent of the big guy, you should rebuke him—lightly. If you are the parent of the little nuisance you should show no sympathy with his plight. Say something like. "Well, if you don't want to get hurt, don't play with the big guys." If you sympathize with him, or if you become the head of his attack team by going on the attack yourself, you will encourage his uncontrolled behavior and you will make your son less popular, thus increasing the probability of his being the target of future attacks.

Kids and young people, especially those of the male variety, have this built in hormonal rush that makes them want to fly through the air, defy danger, go the limit. Kids can't just lazily swing; they have to go as high as they can and then jump out. No boy is ever satisfied with the lowest branch on a tree or the first gear on a bicycle. Skate boards and roller blades are made to be hormone burners. Where there are two boys they will find two sticks and swing them at each other in some sort of imaginary contest.

When my boys were big enough to run, they would take their metal Tonka trucks, and holding them by the sides of the truck-bed they would run down the gravel driveway at full speed. And as if the loud noise of the rattling truck was not enough, they would imitate the sound of a jet airplane. Many a time I had to catch up to them and block their raceway in order to get their attention so I could demand a moment of conversation with someone standing in the yard. When I gave the all-clear signal, they would blast off down the driveway racing each other and banging their trucks together. They learned not to come to me with their bloody hands, elbows, and, occasionally, heads. I showed no sympathy with self-induced wounds. I made them to understand that it was part of the price that must be stoically bore by little boys who chose racing gravel trucks for sport or profit.

I love boys. I like them dirty, rambunctious, grinning, and spontaneous. Although little boys need to learn when and where their exuberance is appreciated. As a pastor, if I were visiting in a home and a little seven-year-old jumped on me to tickle me, I would appreciate the fact that the child liked me enough to be spontaneous. I would also appreciate the mother's embarrassment of her son's wild behavior. Pastors are big enough to take care of themselves.

If his spontaneous exuberance lacks discrimination, train him to properly channel it, but do not turn him into a girl. Invite other boys over and go out to watch them wrestle. I always rooted for the one on the bottom, whether it was my boy or another.

When other boys visited, our boys would yell and run out of the house to get something exciting going. I expected them to climb, jump, wrestle, push, fall, get hurt, and get up to try it all again. Children establish their own social rules. If one goes outside the limits of acceptable push-and-shove the others will respond with discipline.

Your son would have been better left alone. He admitted attacking the bigger fellow. A little thrashing from the big boys would teach him the limits. I would only intervene if I felt that the fight was going to cause serious damage to one of them.

Where do we draw the line in this matter of kids roughing each other? Teach your boys to be kind and loving toward their neighbor. A rule I often repeated was, "Fun is fun as long as everyone is having fun; if not then you are being a bully." Understand, roughhousing by mutual consent is kind and loving, as far as little boys are concerned.

Attitude is the line. Never permit anger, jealously, hostility, wrath, or violence. I taught my boys that if someone becomes angry and wants to fight, you should walk off. Never stay to prove that you are not scared or to settle an argument with a fight. Hostile fighting was always wrong, even when the other guy started it. I taught them to be pacifists in their own defense unless their life or limb was in eminent danger, in which case they could use sufficient force to evade their enemy. Never allow pride to draw you into a confrontation or to keep you in one if it unexpectedly develops.

Boys can be rough and still have big hearts and be kind. If their energy is expended in work and good, clean, active tumbling, they will not be as prone to sudden uncontrolled displays of hyperness.

Again I emphasize, focus on attitude. Come down hard and quick on selfish, mean spirits, but back off and give them room to explode—as long as they are grinning.

Mama, close your eyes. Go back in the house. It is likely to be too much for your sensitive nature. Those boys out there need to get it out of their systems before one of them grows up to become head of the War Department. ☻

Training Fleshy Flesh

O ccasionally we receive criticism about our emphasis that parents should set up training sessions for their children. Our first book on child training, *To Train Up A Child*, contained an illustration of how we trained our children not to touch guns by placing an unloaded and broken gun in the living room where the children could reach it. We carefully watched them. If they touched it, we spanked their hands with a little switch. One to three switchings was sufficient to prevent the little crawlers and toddlers from ever touching a gun.

"You shouldn't tempt your children," we are told. I can understand how a wrong attitude on the part of the parent could turn this into a hostile entrapment, leaving the child feeling used. But this can only happen if the parent is hostile. If your intention is to train your child, not just seek opportunity to punish him, all will be well. Training sessions are not out of the ordinary. All events in a child's life are training. How many times a day do you have to tell a two-year-old "No"? That is a training session. The difference in a happenstance occurrence and one that you premeditate is that the planned "temptation" can be tailor-made and controlled so as to reap the greatest benefit in the shortest period of time with the least amount of effort, and the least stress on the child. The training session should be staged so as to be natural. The child will not know it is staged. In many cases, if the parent is sensitive, an unplanned event can be turned into a training session.

Often the circumstances that naturally arise are so varied and sporadic that the training is more difficult to communicate. If a child occasionally tears the pages out of a book left within his reach, it may be difficult to communicate your desire due to his failure to remember the previous rebuke. It may be confusing to him when he is suddenly disciplined for tearing the pages out of your favorite Bible. But if you place books on the table where he can access them at any time, and you then stand watch closely and prevent him from tearing the pages, the continual reinforcement over one or two days will train him not to tear pages. However, if you allow him to tear up one kind of paper and not another, it may be difficult for him to determine what is off limits and what is available for tearing.

You the trainer must arrange the environment so as to create the maximum effect in your training. Consistency is the key. You cannot allow a child to play with one set of car keys and not pick up other sets he finds lying around. If you want to be assured that he never plays with keys, you must make all keys off limits. This is not done by placing the keys beyond his reach, but by placing keys within his reach and then consistently denying him the pleasure of touching them.

A child of any age can be easily trained to play in a room and touch half of the objects and not the other half. As a parent I am not prepared to spend the time it would take to enforce too broad a scope of continual temptation, but there are a few things like books, keys, guns, vases, dishes, etc. that must be placed off limits by leaving a test case within physical  limits. If you trained a child not to touch books, and then placed all books out of reach, in time the discipline to not tear books would be forgotten. It is having an opportunity to tear and frequently exercising the will to not do so that confirms in the child the no-tear discipline.

I stayed in the home of a grandpa who had trained his little crawling, eleven-month-old granddaughter to handle one shelf of books but not touch the other. She would also ignore the objects on the top of the coffee table but freely access the trinkets on the under side compartment. During the week I stayed with them, I never saw the grandparents rebuke or spank this child. She cheerfully obeyed. The interesting thing was that she was not so obedient when she was in her own home where the mother was lax in discipline and had not set up training sessions.

Take your choice. One home is full of nagging, griping, criticism, constant rebuke and threat with many spankings, and "go to your rooms." The other home is continuously cheerful and ordered because the parents have trained, occasionally using the switch in the training sessions, and have been consistent to demand complete and uninterrupted obedience. You make your home and children what they are. When one buys an automobile that has frequent breakdowns, he says he got a *lemon*. Children don't come to us as lemons. Parents cultivate them into it by grafting their children into the root of their own unstable souls.

There are several great benefits to training. Parents are benefited by taking the time to train and be consistent, because in the long-run it will take less time. Nagging time is slow time. Each moment is drawn out in stress and anxiety. The griper and nagger put in thirty hours a day, where the smiler is always on vacation. I think the aging clock runs faster on people who are always disappointed and anxious. If you want to grow old in a hurry, don't train your children. Develop an adversarial relationship with them by just waiting for them to irritate you to the breaking point, and then show them you mean business by flying off the handle. But if you train your children they will rise up and call you blessed. You will have time to smile, to play with them, to read to them. People will brag about what good kids you have, and you will smile even more. Your kids will brag about what a fine mother they have, and you will get younger. It's worth it to you to train your kids.

Most importantly, the children benefit from being trained. Children have a developing conscience. They are making judgments about themselves, about how they are doing. "Am I a good person? Am I worthy, important? Am I needed? Am I likeable? Do I make people smile, make them happy? Am I of value? Can I succeed, do something worthwhile?" Many children look into their parents' faces and know that it is useless to even try further. "It doesn't matter, I can't do anything right. I am a bad person. Nobody likes me. I have this problem." Later they will say, "You don't understand me. No one listens to me. No one cares. Everybody is a hypocrite."

When they become teenagers they finally find someone who understands them. The rock musicians rapping out cynicism, rebellion, and hate express their feelings. Friends who gather in the dark and indulge the flesh become their family. Parents are "square," out of touch. It's reaping day, parent. And he went from such a nice little boy who was "hyper active" to human trash in just ten years. It happened on your watch. Proper training behind a smile would have prevented this.

If you neglect a garden, it goes to weeds. If you neglect a motor, it seizes up and throws a rod. If you neglect your health, you die. If you neglect your marriage, your partner is miserable and may leave. If you neglect your government, it turns to tyranny. If you neglect your employment, you may be fired. But what if you neglect your children's training? Certainly we cannot expect children to automatically become Christian gentlemen and ladies. Yes, children benefit the most from proper training. There is no alternative.

If you are the parent of a teenager who is in rebellion, you may feel that I have been hard on you. You scream, "Don't just tell me what a failure I have made, tell me what to do to make it right." I am hard on you because there is nothing you can DO to make it right. There are no external principles, no tricks to making it all right. I am hard on you because your greatest need is to repent. You need a broken heart. You need to face the fact that it is all your fault.

When you stop blaming your child, you can eventually win his respect and gain his confidence enough to be invited into his circle of friends. If you cannot earn your way into his inner circle, you are wasting your time trying to control him. Nursing days and threatening days are over. It's person to person now. You have to be real if you would make a real difference. You must become twice the person you want your child to become—twice the patience, twice the love, twice the discipline, twice the kindness, twice the honesty, twice the "I am sorry, will you forgive me?"

We are talking about how children benefit from being trained. Children need the discipline parents can give. They have the will but not the way. Their flesh is weak. It is not just your criticism that weighs them down. Their own consciences are actively critiquing their performances. They feel badly when they don't live up to their own expectations. Parents have the maturity and the will power to provide a suitable structure for their children and to build in them the fortitude to do what they know they ought.

Children have the same inner struggle as adults. Each is a living soul created to glorify God. The need to walk in righteousness is innate in every human being, even children. The human soul cannot find peace unless living to glorify God. This means living benevolently, speaking kindly, and living sacrificially for the sake of one's fellow man.

Yet the flesh of the child stands in opposition to the law of the mind. The flesh of a child, just like the flesh of an adult, wants to indulge. The bodily appetites care nothing for the rule of law or for the needs of others. The flesh wants to be first, get the most, get it all, keep it to the self, and damn anyone who gets in the way. All flesh is self-gratifying and self-consuming. Your child is a living soul in a body of corruptible flesh. When the mind of the child understands duty and knows what it ought to do, the flesh still cries out for fulfillment. Your child does not have the strength to do what he knows he ought. Shades of Romans 7.

The child is inadequate to the challenges of the flesh. The problem arises from the fact that a child is born with all of the fleshly appetites, except one that develops at puberty, but with none of the self-restraint that comes with maturity of intellect. No matter how hungry an adult is, he will not sit in a public place and smear spaghetti all over his face. The mind tempers the flesh for obvious reasons. But the infant cannot relate to any reasons for restraint. So the infant has run-away flesh with a mind that cannot restrain it.

As the understanding develops, children gain an increasing knowledge of their responsibility to govern themselves for the sake of others. They begin to feel a sense of duty to their fellow man. As the soul buds it bears the flower of moral responsibility. Knowledge of good and evil becomes a factor to be reckoned.

This conflict of soul and flesh, with the flesh dominant, is the point at which parents are indispensable. The parents' duty is to assist the child in governing his flesh. Parents must be the child's rule of law, his conscience, his unction and motivation, enforcing self-restraint and discipline. The child will not do this by himself. The two- to ten-year-old needs help possessing his own soul.

The wonderful thing is that the child knows, with an ever increasing degree as he gets older, that he has a duty to be in conformity to God's law. Though he cannot muster the strength of character to make the sacrifices necessary to obey the law of his mind, nonetheless he knows, to some degree, what he ought to do. He knows he should pick up his dirty clothes, do his part in carrying out the garbage. He knows he should not bully his sister. He should not beg and whine. He should not allow his appetite to control him, and he should not make demands in the store. With the increase of age, the child's understanding causes him to hold himself accountable to this unwritten rule of law. His own conscience smarts in pain or relaxes in approval according to how he judges himself to have responded to his duty.

A child's guilt will not drive him to do what he knows he ought. Condemnation from parents compounds the guilt and cause moral isolation, but the flesh still lusts. The feelings of failure will never motivate the child to have the strength of soul to resist the desires of the flesh. Increasingly, the child is carnal, sold under sin.

Enter the parents! Cause your child to do what he knows he ought. He may squawk, drag his feet, and tell you how mean you are, but the flesh must not be allowed to win over the soul. A child caused to submit to authority has an inner witness that this is good. He knows he has done what he ought. He feels good about himself. His flesh is subdued by the powers of your self-restraint. His conscience is satisfied with the freedom of doing what one ought. He is happy when closely governed and disciplined. The rod plays its part in removing the guilt. Parents are running a mini, divine kingdom, sanctifying their children. I get many letters from parents telling of how their miserable, whiney, stubborn child suddenly became happy and began to enjoy everything with a smile after just three days of forced obedience and discipline.

Later in life, if your child is born again, he will have the Holy Spirit to empower him to victory. Until that time, you are all the strength and guidance he is going to have. If you wait until your child is old enough to be born again, so he can deal with his own flesh, by that time he will have a long life of fleshly habits and indulgences ruling his daily life. If you don't provide discipline when he is young, when he is old enough to be saved, he may not want to repent to God. He may love the flesh so much that he does not want God to interfere with his pleasure.

Parents have the privilege of preparing their children to be turned over to the Holy Spirit for the completion of their sanctification. Make your children happy. Teach them to obey. ☺

Drug Addicts

Several years ago many little boys became drug addicts. The little boys' mothers took them to the doctor so he could prescribe the drug for them. The drug is called Ritalin. Addicts purchase it on the streets and use it to get their highs. Professionals use it to control little boys who have not been trained to control themselves. Granted, some little boys need more training and still they are scarcely able to control themselves. But there have been boys down through the ages with this kind of temperament and energy, but only in the last generation have parents resorted to drugs to control their children.

It is a development that could have been predicted, for many of the mothers are drug addicts also. Their drug is called Prozac, or some other name with the same application. It too controls moods, just like Ritalin. There is an herb to take the place of Prozac, it is called St. John's Wort. It is an old drug, a natural drug, but nonetheless a drug. It is sad to look out over a crowd of strong, young families knowing that as many as 1/4 of the mothers over 35 years old are on Prozac, and about the same percentage of squirming little boys are on Ritalin. One psychologist told us that as many as 1/3 of all the young boys in the school system of Texas are on Ritalin. Some schools report as high as 70% of their male students are legally drugged.

When I think of Ritalin or Prozac I think of a great big bandage that is covering up an ugly wound so that no one will see it. Very likely a woman that goes on Prozac today will need to double the dosage in six months, and within two years will need to add another drug to her growing bag of drugs in order to maintain the same results. Drugs are not the answer. God's Word is exceedingly clear on that point. Oh, I know your case is different. One woman says she is so hyper that the drug is needed to keep her calm so she doesn't get physically sick. I heard that on the street long before I heard it from a religious mother. Another woman says she loses control and is so full of anger that her family suffers unless she takes the drug. Still another woman says she is so depressed she is afraid she will end her life without it. One sad fact is these mothers are training their children to be depressed, to feel that violent, angry rage is not sin, but sickness, to depend on a drug instead of obeying God concerning temperance. These little girls are growing up learning and using their mother's excuses. Soon they will need their mother's drug.

So if Prozac is only a bandage, what is the cure? The first step is repentance toward God, taking responsibility for your own actions, moods, and intemperance.

Then take responsibility for your own health. I am not a doctor. I don't have any answers that you couldn't find yourself with a little reading and a lot of question asking. Here is what I have learned. Again, it is only a lay-person's opinion, based on information available at the local library.

For the most part, Prozac seems to be a woman's drug. It appears that mood swings begin to surface somewhere around 33 to 37 years old, at which time Prozac is recommended. Most of the women complain of being tired, and wonder if they have a new disease. These women usually have a history of poor diet, with bouts of constipation or irritable bowels. The physical link seems obvious. The B-complex vitamins are very helpful to restore mood balance, which would indicate that the body is not getting proper nutrition. I share the opinion of others that most physical problems start in the bowels. Just as our sinus cavities when irritated produce mucous to throw off the offending matter, so the bowels have a similar response to toxins. Chemicals in food products, along with white sugar and constipation, cause the bowels to produce protective mucous that eventually forms a thick, rubber-like substance. With the bowels so lined, few nutrients penetrate to where they can be assimilated. When you are young, your colon is still in good operating condition, but around 35 years old the bad habits of youth begin to play havoc. Suddenly the few nutritious foods you do eat are insufficient to feed the failing body.

A good colon cleanse, followed by a careful diet, would greatly help this problem. Take responsibility for your own health. Discipline yourself not to take the fast, easy cure, which leads to greater problems. Drugs are not the answer. In the end you are a "Whole Woman," just like the article we wrote on the "Whole Boy." The answer requires more than just a pill or a chat with a health expert. You must be willing to call sin, sin. Go to the library and learn how to take care of your body; then get out into the sunshine with a heart of thanksgiving, running, jumping, and laughing, whether you feel like it or not. Find some way to minister to others that is both creative and rewarding. Stop playing pity party. That scene will grow tiresome to your children as they get older. Take command of your life. Choices you made caused you to be sick. Now make the choices necessary to be well again. ☺

Dear Michael and Debi,

Greetings in our Saviors name. Well, it has been almost 3 months since I wrote you last and read your book for the first time. What a change that is coming on! I personally feel like I've been pressed through a food grinder at times but I know it will all be worth it in view of eternity! I've had a lot of changing to do on myself and I must admit it has been difficult. I dare even say it was impossible for me to be the Christian wife I needed to be. I wrestled long and hard till one day I fell on my knees and gave it to God. Wow! He can do anything. Since then it has become a lot easier. Now I don't get my feelings hurt at the drop of a hat. I'm not yelling or nagging. Your book *Me? Obey him?* has been a big help. I think my husband is liking the changes, too. He's starting to look at me like he once did when we were first married. It seems as if he's "falling in love" with me again. I try always to greet him with a smile and rejoice in his presence. There is a change coming on!!!...

In Christian Love, GA

Broken Circles

The names and some details have been changed to protect the guilty, but the events are true.

R uth is five years old. Her mother recently left her daddy because he drinks too much. The home life was not good, but it wasn't all bad. It was a small circle that included a warm house, a mama and a daddy, some siblings, and a sense of security. The older siblings were doing well in school, and even though mama and daddy yelled a lot, it was still home. Now little Ruth lives in an apartment with her mommy, although she spends at least three nights a week at home with Daddy. Mommy said she didn't want Daddy to mess them up, so she left him, but she's lonesome and needs to go out, so she asks Daddy to keep the kids more all the time.

If someone asked little Ruth where she lives she would look confused, stare off into space, and finally answer, "With mommy at the apartment." Now her life revolves in two part circles. She has two places to live, she has two authorities, which often disagree, but she no longer has a sense of security—that has been replaced with fear.

Mommy now has a friend. He lives at the apartment with them. He is a strange man and Ruth is uncomfortable around him. She doesn't understand why, but in her tiny, broken circle she no longer feels at home.

Mommy had a date and a baby-sitter came. Mommy didn't

come home until real late and Ruth did not wake up for school. Daddy called, but older brother was afraid to tell him why they weren't at school. The next day all the kids went to stay at Daddy's house. The house is different now. Less furniture, messy, it smells funny, but it's more familiar than the apartment, so it's better. Daddy's friends came over. Mommy doesn't like Daddy's friends. They drink a lot, and one friend wants to hold Ruth, and she is afraid. So much fear, so much uncertainty, so much turmoil.

Children are so flexible; they can take so much and still do just fine. That's what I've always heard from parents who bend their children a lot. When Grandma called she could tell something was wrong, and she told Ruth, "Get outside on the porch with the other kids, I'm coming right now." Ruth feels better. Grandma's house was once a place to visit and eat candy, but now it is another partial circle, a safe partial circle, warmly secure with Grandma and Papa, the same house with the same stuff in it. And Grandma is always the same. There's no fear there, but it is not Ruth's house, only another partial circle in her ever widening flow of circles—now that the real circle is broken.

Ruth is learning to use her circles. If she doesn't like doing something she can just cry and say she wants Daddy. If Daddy will not let her have something, she can just beg to go stay with Mommy. If she has to go to school when she doesn't want to, she can be sick and ask for Grandma. Ruth has learned that where there is more than one circle there is really no circle at all. No authority, no security, the only absolute is what Ruth wants. Ruth has no one to protect her from herself, from her own lusts. Grandma can be a loving grandparent protecting her from the bad guys at Daddy's house. Daddy can make her feel happy. Mommy can love her, but the authority has been given into her tiny hands by default.

Several years pass. When Ruth was a little girl, Grandma's house was a place of security, but now that Ruth is thirteen years old, it is just a dull, boring, old place. Candy bars and TV no longer satisfy her appetite. Her flesh has grown, and with it has grown the habit of getting what she wants. Over the years she has learned how to cover her tracks when she wants the freedom to have some fun. She tells Dad, "I'm at Grandma's," and tells Mom, "I'm spending the weekend at Dad's." She tells Grandma, "Dad said I could stay over with friend Marsha." The tight circle that God placed her in to protect and guard her was removed by Mommy's and Daddy's sin.

Ruth has been left uncovered.

Some parents rip that covering off their children, not by divorce, but by disagreement in policy. A mother will whisper to her daughter, "You can go, but don't you dare tell Dad you did." That daughter has lost her covering for all times and all occasions. Mother has taken it from Daddy as well as from herself. Some daddies give it away. Daughter begs, gets angry, yells, pleads, and Daddy finally yells, "Just get out of here, I don't care what you do, just give me some peace." Daughter learned this from Mama. Then some daddies just pretend they don't notice; after all, Daddy's little girl has always done real well. Daddy wants to be the sweetheart. He gives his girls complete freedom so "they'll know I trust them." Poor little girls grow up doing "what is right in their own eyes."

Little girls and boys need a complete, secure circle in order to grow up well adjusted. God designed that the man should be strong and wise as the head of his wife. A girl, having spent her entire youth growing up with a daddy that watched over and protected her in her day-to-day activities, will be ready to assume her role as a wife that will bring honor to God and her husband. So many little girls are growing up today without that circle of protection and authority. They grow up with fears and insecurities on top of the rebellion and fleshly indulgence. When they enter marriage they don't know how to be submissive, confident wives because they never were submissive, confident little girls to their daddies. The only way they can find fulfillment is by "doing what's right in their own eyes."

A great majority of women are depressed, discouraged, angry, and totally out of control in their flesh. They live in some kind of a silly fantasyland. To make matters worse, their husbands are selfish, defeated sissies. Soul sickness is at epidemic proportions. Divorce is a terrible crime against all. And not only divorce, but also the spirit of defiance, of "getting my rights," is quickly destroying any hope of happiness.

Many women will read this and say, "I knew I was doomed from the start, so why try, it is my parents' fault." It is true your parents did fail you, but now you stand before God to give an answer for your own sin. It's no good crying over spilled milk. It's time to get a cloth and clean up the mess, being careful not to create any more spills. Are you content to continue passing this burden down to your children? Each person stands before God either to obey or to dishonor. Because of your up-bringing you might have a propensity to be selfish, get angry, or to manipulate your surroundings, but it is ultimately your choice to obey God or not. As you seek God and seek to obey His Word you will begin to mature in the way God meant for you to mature while you were growing up. When God says in His Word for the woman to reverence her husband it will not seem like an archaic translation. When the Scripture says Sara called her husband "lord," it will not appear sacrilegious.

So, mama, are you unhappy with that selfish, "no-good" husband of yours? God has made a way, and His way is still your only way to raise your little girls to become honorable little mamas. The way to raise obedient, serving little girls is by example. How you treat Daddy will in a great degree decide how they will respond to authority, and ultimately to God. You can't change Daddy, but you can change your side of the world.

Do you treat your husband with affection, but little honor or respect? Do you slip behind his back to go shopping, or waste your days reading romance novels? When you dishonor him, you dishonor God. He knows it, you know it, and your children know it. You limit God's blessing in your life.

The slide is down hill. Every child is selfish, and will get more selfish. As parents we need to seek to obey God against all odds; that's what sanctification is all about. Our job as mothers starts with being good wives. Your role as mother will go no further than how you fulfill your role as wife. When parents break their own circle, they break their children's circle as well. Neither broken marriages nor broken relationships produce whole children.

Even when all goes well our children will not be perfect. They will have their own hurts and weaknesses to overcome. But they don't need to start life handicapped by dragging along the added burden of the sins of their parents. Life will throw enough mud at the children without them leaving home carrying a load provided by parents.

There is still an abundance of grace and love to be poured on those who will repent toward God. When you lay yourself on God's altar, your children reap the blessings of the sacrifice. When we flush the garbage out of our own lives, our children experience the cleansing. ☺

Seeing Through a Glass Darkly

T wenty-two years ago a wonderful, sweet, darling two-year-old boy, whom I loved, came down with a fever. Within 24 hours he was dead. During the days after his death, while the family grieved, I kept his baby brother. I re-member staring at my sweet Rebekah and feeling a sense of relief that it was not she who was taken.

"When I was a child, I spake as a child, I understood as a child, I thought as a child: but when I became a man, I put away childish things." What I am about to say will be hard for many of you to understand, but as an older woman I feel compelled to speak.

Death is not the worst enemy. When I was a young mother, this truth was simply beyond comprehension. To lose a child was my worst fear. I avoided long bridges because I was afraid I could not save all my children if the car plunged into the water. I carefully chose cars by the ease of opening the safety buckles and doors—just in case. I studied medications, familiarizing myself with potential problems and learning how to use alternative medicines. My natural instinct to protect my children, regardless of the cost, was in full operation. God gave me that instinct. Along the way, other children whom I knew died, and I continued to cling to my children, trying to guard their safety. Yet how frail my efforts would have been if death had come calling.

When you are young and raising a family, death seems to be the ultimate loss. Their grief is a pain you can only know first hand. When we are young, we see through a glass darkly. As we grow older, life is not as big as we thought it was when it was all before us. Life in this flesh is quite temporary. I am not so old yet. Life is still precious. Death is still the enemy. I continue to cling to life, not only my own, but to that of those I love. Yet, my clinging has changed. Somewhere over the passing years I realized death was not the worst enemy. Grief over death stopped being the worst grief. I can now see just a tiny bit clearer through the dark glass.

Eternity is so eternal, so terribly final, so completely forever. Death is not final. By the grace of God, it is not without hope. There is something yet beyond. Temporarily saying goodbye, even to a child, is still temporary. There will be a glad tomorrow. At the parting of death it is our own loss we grieve, not the child's, who has gone into the presence of God. But there is a loss into the darkness of eternity that is far more than the loss of temporary separation.

The older you get, the more you see the real enemy; you learn to recognize the real grief. It is not a temporary parting that brings apprehension, but knowledge of certain and eternal judgment awaiting your child. The pain of that rebellious child seeking a life of destruction is a thousand times more grievous than losing a baby. That mother I spoke of earlier, the one who lost her baby, suffered another, far greater loss years later. She lost her second son to the devil. Looking back, she now admits it was her own selfish grief and bitterness. It stole her joy, leaving her without a smile to nurture her living son. I heard her say 14 years after the death of her son, "It would have been easier to have also lost this one to death as a baby than to see what has become of him now."

I remember when I carried my first child in my womb; I had waited for 3 years, and when I finally got pregnant I was the happiest person I had ever known. One day, as I practiced childbirth relaxation, God spoke to me. I believe He told me to give the child I was carrying to Him. I began to cry and beg God not to take the baby; all afternoon I wrestled with my own feelings and what I believed God wanted of me. Finally, in great grief I surrendered the child to God. As the days passed, I was totally thrilled and amazed that nothing happened. When the baby was born strong and healthy, I knew God had something bigger than what I had feared. Still, I saw through a glass darkly. Life and death were the only two "biggies" in my life.

Thereafter, as each child was conceived, I eagerly gave it to God. Throughout their childhood I had instincts just like every other mother. I would protect my children at any cost. Instinct, although an overwhelming feeling, is just instinct. Even mother animals will die protecting their young. Oh, mother, if we as young mothers could just get a vision of something greater than instinct for our children, and begin to feel just as urgently for their souls, how different it would make us. As young mothers, if we could have eternity in our eyes, many things that appear as tragedies would not be so tragic. Older mothers, God-fearing mothers see more clearly. Whether it is age or spiritual maturity, I don't know—maybe both— but it is not for their lives we fear; it for their souls. We are still stirred to pray for their safety and health, but our consuming prayer is that they overcome all the snares and diversions this evil world can offer. Where once a mother begged God's protection for her child, she now begs Divine intervention at any cost (including life or limb). No, death is not your greatest enemy. Death brings a temporary sadness, a time of great loneliness, but in Christ there is always hope. Your greatest enemies are those vying for your child's soul.

People often ask me how I could ever let my daughter Rebekah go to the mountains of Papua New Guinea. What they don't understand is that I let Rebekah go years before when she was still in my womb. Yes, I have fears, but there is great hope. There is great joy. There is wonderful peace in knowing this is only temporary. I shall see her in a few months, or maybe in a few years, but most assuredly I will be with her again. There is no grief, there is no pain, there is only a glad tomorrow. Yes, I cry when she leaves, and I wander from room to room for a few weeks. When there is word she will return I clean and clean, and buy her clothes and talk and cry some more.

But, mother, what would it be like if she were to disappear from home, leaving in anger and rebellion? If I knew she left with a man I didn't like or respect. Weeks pass and there is no word, there is no hope. Grief? That is real grief. You think because they are grown you cease to feel? Death is such a simple thing compared to this grief. You lose a child to death, and everyone understands your sorrow and shares your pain. But lose a child to Satan's grip and you are an island alone, buffeted on every side with such turmoil, such pain, sleepless nights, exhausted prayer, hopelessness. Grief? Only the older mother understands eternal grief. Only the older mother can look in the face of a young mother and say, train your children to obey, raise them to love God, be real in the home, so much depends on it.

When you are a young mother raising a family, it is so easy to care about your own feelings, your own hurts, your little fuss with your husband. Oh, but Mother, there is coming a day when your own feelings, hurts, and fusses will seem so immaterial, so silly. It is that atmosphere emanating from your relationship to your husband, your attitude and responses that help decide your baby's future in eternity. It is not your child training techniques; it is who you are today. It is how you respond to life's ups and downs and to life's grief and joy. It is how you honor your husband, thus how you honor God.

We go through life so protective of our children's bodies. Let us as mothers early look to the protection of their souls. The enemy is not death. The enemy is not outside, lurking to get in; the enemy is a mother's heart dedicated to a mother's feelings. It is our own selfishness, our own anger, our own bitterness, and our own disappointments. The enemy is Mother, doing what is right in her own eyes instead of obeying God. God, grant us the wisdom to get beyond instinct to the wisdom of true love. God, grant us hearts to see, to feel, and to live with eternity in our eyes.

"The aged women likewise, that...they may teach the young women to be sober, to love their husbands, to love their children (Titus 2: 3-4)." ☺

Dear Debi,
Thank you so much for "setting me free" from curriculum slavery. Your tape, *Best Homeschooling Ideas,* is wonderful! I was a slave lesson planner and a bully to my girls. My whole family thanks you. Your book, *To Train Up A Child,* saved our family. I am excited to share your message with my homeschool friends.
    J. P.

Index

No Greater Joy

After writing this book, the Pearls began publishing No Greater Joy, a free bimonthly magazine, as an offshoot of To Train Up A Child. It was created to answer questions not addressed in To Train Up A Child, and explore relevant and broader issues outside the scope of the book.

The articles appearing in No Greater Joy have been compiled into these three volumes. Each one contains numerous insightful, instructive and practical articles on the subject of child training, family relationships and homeschooling.

These products, as well as many others, can be purchased through our website at www.nogreaterjoy.org or write to us requesting a FREE sample magazine which contains a list of our products and order form.

No Greater Joy Vol. 1

Reprints of the first two years of No Greater Joy articles. Covers the subjects of sibling rivalvy, pouting, bad attitudes, and much more.

No Greater Joy Vol. 2

Let your children listen to great bedtime stories. Covers the subjects of rowdy boys, homeschooling, grief, and much more.

No Greater Joy Vol. 3

Children learn wisdom and enjoy listening to the stories as you read to them volumes 1, 2, and 3. Covers the subjects of marriage relationships and how they affect children, joy, much more.

FREE Magazine Subscription

No Greater Joy Ministries Inc. publishes a bimonthly magazine with answers to questions received in the mail. Send us your name and mailing address and we will put you on our mailing list. Your information is confidental. We do not share your information with anyone. If you are on our mailing list, you will also receive notification of when the Pearls are speaking in your area.

You can also read additional material on our website www.nogreaterjoy.org or you can sign up on our website to receive No Greater Joy.

NGJ is a 501(c)3 Non-profit orginization dedicated to serving families with the good news of Jesus Christ.

Other books by the Pearls:

To Train Up A Child
No Greater Joy Vol. 1
No Greater Joy Vol. 2
No Greater Joy Vol. 3
Created to be His Help Meet
Romans - Commentary
By Divine Design
Repentance
To Betroth or Not to Betroth
Pornography–Road to Hell

In Defense of *Biblical* Chastisement
Holy Sex
Baptism in Jesus' Name
Justification and the book of James
1 John 1:9 the Protestant Confessional

No Greater Joy Ministries Inc.
1000 Pearl Road
Pleasantville TN 37033
United States of America
www.nogreaterjoy.org